Expeditions of Honour

Expeditions of Honour

The Journal of John Salusbury
in Halifax, Nova Scotia, 1749–53

Edited by Ronald Rompkey

Newark: University of Delaware Press

London and Toronto: Associated University Presses

© 1982 by Associated University Presses, Inc.

Associated University Presses, Inc.
4 Cornwall Drive
East Brunswick, N.J. 08816

Associated University Presses Ltd
27 Chancery Lane
London WC2A 1NF, England

Associated University Presses
Toronto M5E 1A7, Canada

Library of Congress Cataloging in Publication Data

Salusbury, John, 1707–1762.
  Expeditions of honour.

  Bibliography: p.
  Includes index.
  1. Nova Scotia—History—1713–1763. 2. Nova
Scotia—Description and travel. 3. Halifax, N. S.—
History. 4. Halifax, N. S.—Description.
5. Salusbury, John, 1707–1762. 6. British in
Halifax, N. S.—Biography. I. Rompkey, Ronald.
II. Title.
F1038.S2 1980   971.6′01   79-13797
ISBN 0-87413-169-3

For my mother, Margaret Rompkey

Contents

Preface

As J. B. Brebner demonstrated in *New England's Outpost* (1927), the Anglo-French confrontation on the isthmus of Chignecto in the early 1750s was part of a complex British plan to govern the Acadian population of Nova Scotia, a modest prelude to the important victories at Louisbourg in 1758 and Québec in 1759. The narrow isthmus was a testing point for the claims of two imperial powers engaged in a continental struggle that continued uninterrupted during the interval between the signing of the Treaty of Aix-la-Chapelle (1748) and the beginning of the Seven Years' War (1756). During this confusing period of official "peace," the times seemed out of joint. There were no rules to play by, though the game of territorial influence continued unabated. While the apprehensions, fears, and disasters it produced preoccupied soldiers and civilians on both sides, we are fortunate that a few took the trouble to record their adventures, as Dr. J. C. Webster noted over forty years ago in publishing the diary of John Thomas and the journal of Louis de Courville. Already available, he said, were the journals of Joshua Winslow, John Winslow, Abijah Willard, Jacau de Fiedmont, Hon. Robert Monckton, and Thomas Pichon. And we may now add to this list of adventurers the name of John Salusbury, a rather reluctant participant thrust into the midst of events in Halifax and Chignecto by virtue of a patronage appointment from the earl of Halifax, president of the Board of Trade and Plantations. Unlike his fellow journalists, Salusbury adopts the point of view of a virtual outsider, for from the time of his arrival in Governor Cornwallis's entourage, he was content to stay out of the way while a form of government was being established in Halifax and lucrative commercial arrangements were being developed by New England merchants. While the Halifax authorities denied him important information and the secretary saw to it that his employments were "curtail'd dayly," Salusbury attacked them secretly in his journal and letters. Though he might not have betrayed his resentment publicly, he left no doubt about it in his private memoranda, where his two terms of exile in Nova Scotia became "expeditions of honour" and the town of Halifax itself the "vortex of Dullness."

I first became interested in John Salusbury several years ago when I was collecting information for a study of Soame Jenyns, an eighteenth-century poet and Whig politician, and attempting to trace my ancestors, a family of Palatines who emigrated to Halifax in 1750 as part of a scheme to encourage the settling of "foreign Protestants." These two interests came together during a discussion I had with the late Professor James L. Clifford, biographer of Salusbury's daughter, Hester Thrale (Piozzi), about whether Mrs. Thrale's companion, Dr. Samuel Johnson, had read the journal while he was examining Mrs. Salusbury's papers after her death. My own examination of the papers yielded no clear evidence of Johnson's hand. Instead, I discovered that Salusbury provided a unique perspective from which to observe the founding of Halifax amidst the machinations of the British and French disputants. With Professor Clifford's encouragement, I then set about editing the seven small memorandum books preserved in the John Rylands University Library of Manchester (Rylands Eng. MS 615) and the letters to Salusbury's wife, Hester (Rylands Eng. MS 530). A further Salusbury letter bearing upon the trial of Thomas Power (Rylands Eng. MS 655, 9) was later added to the collection.

It seems to me that Salusbury began the journal as a simple memorandum book, though he might have used his notes to report privately to Lord Halifax on the progress of the settlement. As he progressed, he widened his focus to include impressions of political events and personalities, maintaining the right-hand pages for his chronology and reserving the left-hand pages to reflect on it or jot down personal details. Rather than follow Salusbury's unsystematic sequence, I have set off the contents of the left-hand pages in indented sections immediately below the passages with which they are connected. As far as possible, I have presented the text as it appears in the manuscript, altering spelling or punctuation only where the original is confusing. Where words have changed their meanings substantially, I have provided a contemporary gloss from Dr. Johnson's dictionary of 1755 or from the *Oxford English Dictionary*. Illegible words have been bracketed and queried; actual gaps where the page is torn or ink has run have been measured and bracketed. Where there are gaps in the narrative, I have supplemented the text with footnotes based on public documents so as to identify significant persons or events. Some of these persons have never been identified before; others who figure prominently in the later history of Nova Scotia and elsewhere receive fuller biographical treatment in Appendix B.

I am grateful to the John Rylands University Library of Manchester for permission to publish the manuscript and to the British Library, the Public Record Office, and the National Maritime Museum, Greenwich, for their assistance with the research. In Canada, I owe a debt of thanks to the Public Archives of Canada (especially Peter Bower), the National Library of Canada, and the Public Archives of Nova Scotia (especially Brian Cuthbertson and Lois Kernaghan). I must also acknowledge the valuable advice of historians Julian Gwyn, Donald Chard, and W. A. B. Douglas, all of whom read portions of the work in draft. Finally, I wish to thank the Canada Council for the awarding of summer research grants, without which this undertaking would not have been completed.

Acknowledgments

Alfred A. Knopf, Inc., for permission to quote from *The British Empire Before the American Revolution*, vol. 3, by L. H. Gipson.

The Bodley Head Ltd. for permission to quote from *Doctor Johnson and Mrs. Thrale*, by A. M. Broadley.

The British Library, Department of Manuscripts, for permission to quote from B.L. Add. MS. 35,913.

Haynes Publishing Group Ltd. for permission to quote from *Dr. Johnson's Mrs. Thrale*, ed. A. Hayward and J. H. Lobban.

Her Majesty's Stationery Office for permission to quote from *The House of Commons, 1715–1754*, by Romney Sedgwick, and from the *Journal of the Commissioners for Trade and Plantations*.

The John Rylands University Library of Manchester for permission to publish extracts from various papers in the Salusbury Collection.

Methuen & Co. Ltd. for permission to use material from *The Dunciad* (Twickenham Edition, vol. 5), by Alexander Pope, ed. J. Sutherland.

Minister of Supply and Services, Canada, for permission to reproduce excerpts from *Documents Relating to Currency, Exchange and Finance in Nova Scotia with Prefatory Documents, 1675–1758*, ed. Adam Shortt, V. K. Johnston, and Gustave Lanctot.

The New Brunswick Museum for permission to quote from *The Journal of Joshua Winslow*, ed. J. C. Webster.

Oxford University Press for permission to quote from *Thraliana*, by H. L. Piozzi, ed. Katherine Balderston, 2d ed., and from *The Spectator*, ed. Donald F. Bond.

The Public Archives of Nova Scotia for permission to publish an extract from the *Report of the Board of Trustees of the Public Archives of Nova Scotia* (1971).

The Public Record Office for permission to quote material from the CO series and the ADM series.

The United Society for the Propagation of the Gospel for permission to quote from the S.P.G. reports.

Yale University Press for permission to quote from *Hogarth: His Life, Art, and Times*, by Ronald Paulson.

Introduction

The province of Nova Scotia was the youngest and the favourite child of the board. Good God! What sums the nursing of that ill-thriven, hard-visaged, and ill-favoured brat, has cost to this wittol nation? Sir, this colony has stood us in a sum of not less than seven hundred thousand pounds. To this day it has made no repayment.

—Edmund Burke[1]

The Fourteenth Colony

It would be difficult to underestimate the implications of the British victory in America at the end of the Seven Years' War, a victory that imposed a military if not a social solution upon the vexing question of colonial boundaries that had strained Anglo-French diplomatic relations throughout the first half of the eighteenth century. If the French had won, their control of the continental interior would have effectively blocked British expansion westward, and the history of Canada and the United States would now be fundamentally different. Instead, the British victory eliminated the boundary dispute altogether and concluded years of unsatisfactory negotiation that had brought British and French settlers into daily conflict along the coastlines and footpaths of Acadia.

The first attempt at a negotiated settlement, the Treaty of Utrecht (1713), ceded to England all of Hudson Bay, Acadia, Newfoundland, and Saint Christopher in the West Indies. A joint commission was charged with determining the actual boundaries of the British and French territories, but although it met in 1719, it made no progress. While the boundaries remained open to question, American affairs intruded more

15

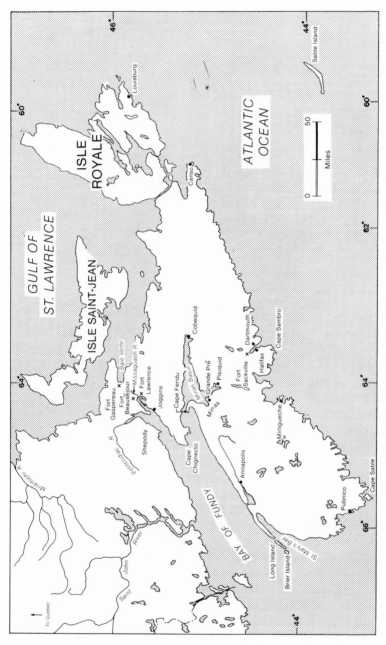

Nova Scotia in 1753. Produced by the Department of Technical Services, University of Alberta.

frequently into the relationship between the two countries at the international level. Meanwhile, the Acadians successfully resisted the feeble British presence at Annapolis Royal with the help of their Micmac allies, frustrating the British plan to govern them.[2] By 1748, when the Treaty of Aix-la-Chapelle compelled Britain to return to France the island of Cape Breton with its fortress at Louisbourg, the British found themselves outflanked. The fortress could now serve as a base for cultivating the loyalty of the Acadians and the Indian tribes of Acadia and New England. Repeating the solution of 1713, the two powers left the boundary question to a joint commission, though they did not name their representatives until 1749.[3] Once more their deliberations dragged on for several years without reaching a satisfactory agreement.[4] At this point, the British government attempted a new and expensive initiative to encourage settlement elsewhere in Acadia.

For years the Board of Trade and Plantations had aimed at transforming Nova Scotia from a military to a civilian colony, partly to draw off settlers from the colony of Massachusetts Bay and partly to satisfy merchant groups and speculators. With the appointment of the duke of Bedford as secretary of the southern department and the earl of Halifax as president of the Board of Trade and Plantations, this project suddenly became a priority in 1748.[5] The harbor of Chebucto, big enough to anchor a whole fleet and strategically located between Annapolis and Louisbourg, would be the new focus of British interest. A link with Annapolis would be established, forts would be built near pockets of Acadian confrontation, and troops forced to evacuate Louisbourg would be deployed to protect settlers. To be effective, though, the plan would have to be put into operation before the French reasserted themselves at Louisbourg. Halifax stressed the urgency of it when he wrote Bedford in 1748:

The only Means of preserving this Country is by a well regulated Settlement of it, and I believe your Grace will be of Opinion, that no Time should be lost in the Performance of this publick Service. It has already been too long delayed, for if it had been undertaken as it ought to have been soon after the Treaty of Utrecht, this Nation would many years ago have felt the happy Effects of it, and particularly in the late War. If it be longer neglected, it possibly never may, it probably never will be in Our Power to effect it, & I take the present Consideration to be no other than whether We shall settle or whether We shall lose the Province of Nova Scotia.[6]

But by the spring of 1749, Parliament had given its approval to the enterprise and the Board of Trade was already busy organizing the details of population and supply. Since Parliament had voted what it considered sufficient funds and a pool of sailors, soldiers, and artificers made redundant by the peace of 1748 was available to serve as a population base, early in March the Board invited settlers with an announcement in the *London Gazette* and similar exhortations in popular magazines.[7]

To the ordinary citizen with no prospect of a secure living in Britain, these advertisements must have suggested a glimpse of the Promised Land, for the Board offered fifty acres of land in fee simple (absolute possession) to every private soldier or seaman and an extra ten acres for every member of his family. (Officers could receive more, depending on their rank.) This grant would also be free from quitrents or taxes for ten years, and at the end of that period no one would be required to pay more than a shilling per annum for every fifty acres granted. In addition, each settler would receive subsistence during the passage and for twelve months after his arrival. That was not all. He would also be furnished with any necessary arms and ammunition and provided with tools for the erection of houses, the cultivation of land, fishing, husbandry, or any other purpose for his support. Standing in a London street, a prospective settler could visualize himself as a virtual guest of the government for a year with few responsibilities, and many of the unemployed found it difficult to resist. In the popular imagination, Nova Scotia became a kind of Utopia where class distinction dissolved, the common miseries of life faded from the memory, and riches abounded in vast expanses of land. Such exaggerations provoked an assortment of satirical verse, and pieces like this "ballad" from the *Gentleman's Magazine* ridiculed the promoters' offerings:

Let's away to *New Scotland*, where Plenty sits queen
O'er as happy a country as ever was seen;
And blesses her subjects, both little and great,
With each a good house, and a pretty estate.

There's wood, and there's water, there's wild fowl and tame;
In the forest good ven'son, good fish in the stream,
Good grass for our cattle, good land for our plough
Good wheat to be reap'd, and good barley to mow.

No landlords are there the poor tenants to teaze,
No lawyers to bully, nor stewards to seize:
But each honest fellow's a landlord, and dares
To spend on himself the whole fruit of his cares.

They've no duties on candles, no taxes on malt,
Nor do they, as we do, pay sauce for their salt:
But all is as free as in those times of old,
When poets assure us the age was of gold.[8]

In another song forming part of a garland dedicated to Nova Scotia, a weaver's wife successfully resists the urgings of her sister, a maid. She refuses to leave her husband and run away to "glorious Nova Scotia" even though, she is told,

Good old Gin there be in Plenty,
Money never can be scanty,
In a Place that is so plenty
    As is *Nova Scotia*:
Leave the Town now I say,
Your Sot like Husband disobey;
Consult your Interest while you may,
    And make for *Nova Scotia*.

Servant Maids that kiss your Masters,
Who lie under great Disasters;
Ne'er fear Fortune ever after,
    Away for *Nova Scotia*:
There you will in splendor live,
And as Maids they'll you receive;
No Ill-thoughts, I pray, believe
    Of generous *Nova Scotia*.[9]

Even more pointed is one of its companion songs. Here a ship's captain lately returned from the colony describes an island of pleasure in the North Atlantic where the rivers run with wine. Streets are paved with mutton pies, walls are made of hasty pudding, and houses are tiled with pancakes:

There is nothing there but Holidays,
    With Musick out of Measure;
Who can forbear to speak the Praise
    Of such a Land of Pleasure:
There you may lead a pleasant Life,
    Free from all Kind of Labour,
And he that is without a Wife,
    May borrow of his Neighbour.

There is no Law nor Lawyers Fees,
    All Men are free from Fury,
For every Man doth what he please,
    Without a Judge or Jury.
The Summer Time is warm they say,
    The Winter is never Colder,
They have no Landlord's Rent to pay,
    Each Man is a Freeholder.[10]

In spite of these scornful amusements, however, hundreds of settlers recognized what seemed to be a comfortable situation and signed on. In the weeks after Governor Cornwallis dropped his anchor in Chebucto harbor, they confronted the wilderness with an air of cheerfulness and determination.

Immediately, more vessels appeared, some laden with troops and civilians evacuated from Louisbourg and others bearing hopeful settlers from New England. The first tree hit the ground. Tents dotted the shoreline, and space for a town expanded into the forest behind them.[11] As though fulfilling the prophecies of the Board of Trade, enthusiastic reports found their way into print. At the end of July, a settler wrote,

> We have already cleared about 20 acres of land, and every one has a hut by his tent. Our work goes on briskly, and the method of employing the people in ship's companies has a good effect in creating an emulation amongst us, every one striving who shall do most; and as the governor is preparing to lay out the lots of land, we shall soon have a very convenient and pleasant town built, which is to be called *Halifax*, in honour of that great and noble lord, to whom this settlement owes its beginning; and from whose well-known and indefatigable zeal for the honour and interest of his country, we hope in time to become a most useful and flourishing colony.[12]

In August, one of his neighbors could confidently predict,

> what people may think in *England* of this settlement, I know not; but so far I can say in its favour, without partiality, that it will be, in a very few years, a flourishing place; for there are all the allurements in the world for inhabitants to come and settle here. The climate is healthful, and more so than in *England*. The soil is fertile and capable of producing all manner of grain and roots, and here is fresh water and rivers in the greatest abundance.[13]

Indeed, the euphoria continued through the first few weeks as the settlers progressed with clearing land and erecting temporary quarters. But if Nova Scotia promised bountiful and salubrious surroundings, it could not guarantee social equality. Too many British people, including those shelved by the navy and the army, were looking for an easy year of it. The New Englanders, on the other hand, were used to conditions in the New World: some had fought with provincial reg-

iments at Annapolis and Louisbourg or in the colonies further south, and others had been busy extending their well-
established commercial network. It was they who would
dominate the civil appointments and business while the
British took a more humble role.

As he prepared for his first winter in North America, Edward Cornwallis, the thirty-six-year-old governor, assessed
the 3,500 settlers he had taken with him and received a shock.
Only a small proportion, he discovered, could support him
adequately, and he wrote worriedly to the Board of Trade:

> Of Soldiers there is only 100—of Tradesmen Sailors &
> others able & willing to work not above 200 more—the rest
> are poor idle worthless vagabonds that embraced the op-
> portunity to get provisions for one Year without labour,
> or Sailors that only wanted a passage to New
> England—Many have come as into a Hospital, to be cured,
> Some of Venereal Disorders, some even incurables—I
> mention this particularly to Your Lordships, because I find
> by experience, that these idle abandond fellows are the
> most troublesome & mutinous & instead of helping hinder
> the rest as much as they can—[14]

Cornwallis's chaplain, William Tutty, a missionary dispatched
by the Society for the Propagation of the Gospel, described
those who embarked from England as nothing more than "a
set of profligate Wretches" debilitated by drink.[15] One of
their own countrymen reported that they were "generally
tumultuous, refractory, full of discontent and murmurings,
capricious in demanding favours, not long satisfied with present concessions, and not seldom abusing them by a restless
importunity for more."[16] "You must send more Troops, &
good Industrious Settlers," Secretary Hugh Davidson petitioned the Colonial Office. "Lord what Scoundrels are
here!—one industrious Man is worth 100 of them—"[17] They
deserted and they died of cold or starvation. Some did not
take the trouble to settle at all.[18] The New Englanders, on the
other hand, were more ambitious and dependable. Joshua
Mauger, a Jerseyman who had moved his business to Halifax
from Louisbourg, explained to the Board of Trade in

January 1750 that the New Englanders "chiefly intended a fishery, and were people of substance, and many did not accept the Governor's allowances except lots of land. . . . "[19] They were businessmen and administrators with an eye to new opportunities but in William Tutty's opinion, they behaved pretentiously in their religious observances and prevaricated in their dealings. "Tho they seek the Lord often (to use an Expression very common and familiar with them) yet they seek him in such a manner as makes it very difficult to find him," he told his superiors.[20] "As Treasurer," wrote Hugh Davidson, "I have to do with the most troublesome people on Earth, the N. England Merchants—You can have no notion of their meanness & Extortion—200 pr Ct is all the profit they ask."[21]

Not surprisingly, though, these were the very people Cornwallis selected to serve as his council members and his principal salaried officials. With two exceptions, the men he chose had either sat on the previous council at Annapolis or demonstrated their skills at Louisbourg or New England. Paul Mascarene had been president of the council at Annapolis in the absence of the governor; Edward How had also been an Annapolis councillor, but his experience extended to a variety of other activities as well; John Gorham, a member of a distinguished New England family, had commanded provincial troops at Annapolis; Benjamin Green, appointed Naval Officer, was a New Englander who had accompanied Sir William Pepperrell to Louisbourg and had later become secretary to the council there.[22] Other officials such as Benjamin Ives (Captain of the Port), William Foye (Provost Marshal) and Otis Little (Commissary of Stores) were seasoned colonists, and in addition to these there were influential merchants like Joshua Mauger and ships' captains like John Rous who were already well known at Louisbourg and Annapolis. Two other councillors received patronage appointments. Hugh Davidson, a friend of Richard Aldworth, undersecretary of state to the duke of Bedford, received the important dual position of secretary and treasurer, and John Salusbury, through the influence of Lord Halifax, was given the title "Register and Receiver of His Majesty's Rents."[23] Neither found favor with Governor Cornwallis. Davidson was suspected of trading with government stores for his own profit, and after Cornwallis sent him to England to explain his actions to the board in September 1750, he never returned. As for Salusbury, he seems to have been the victim of a conflict between Cornwallis and the Board of Trade. The governor did not consider the Registry to be an essential part of the secretary's office, but their Lordships did.[24] The result was that though the position stayed, Cornwallis delayed swearing Salusbury in until August 1749 and virtually ignored him from then on.

As his journal shows, John Salusbury was sensitive and intelligent, but unsympathetic to what was going on around him in Halifax. He had not chosen to go there in the first place. Destitute through ill fortune and bad management, he was being given a second chance, at the age of forty-one,[25] to achieve some success in his life. As the youngest son of a landed Welsh family of ancient origin, he had found his present employment only through his links with the patronage system. To some, Nova Scotia offered the chance for preferment or profit. To Salusbury, it was an unavoidable inconvenience. He did not so much choose this new career as acquiesce in an arrangement contrived by his family and friends beginning in the summer of 1748, when he moved his wife and infant daughter to London. Dr. Edward Crane, the new prebendary of Westminster, introduced Salusbury to Lord Halifax, whose family Crane served as tutor.[26] Crane, it seems, was an unusually influential figure in Halifax's household. The playwright Richard Cumberland, later Halifax's private secretary, wrote:

A better guide and more faithful counsellor he could not have, for amongst all the men it has been my chance to know, I do not think I have known a calmer, wiser, more right-headed man; in the ways of the world, the politics of the time and the characters of those, who were in the public management and responsiblity of affairs, Doctor Crane was incomparably the best steersman, that his pupil could take his course from, and so long as he submitted to his temperate guidance he could hardly go astray. The opinions of Doctor Crane were on all points decisive.[27]

The settlement of Nova Scotia preoccupied Halifax as soon as he was appointed president of the Board of Trade in November 1748. Distributing colonial offices without the board's approval was not an unusual practice for him,[28] and when Crane recommended that Salusbury accompany Cornwallis, he had no trouble finding him a place under his direct patronage. The idea did not interest Salusbury at first, but rather than face the embarrassment of turning down a firm offer, he accepted and reluctantly set sale in Cornwallis's ship in May 1749. Crane wrote that summer, "we think much of you, talk much of you & expect much from you."[29] Halifax assured him that "if there is any thing in which I can be serviceable to you, pray inform me of it, and I shall gladly obey your commands."[30] But arriving in Halifax, Salusbury took no further advantage of Halifax's favor. He was a lonely and embittered man.

During the first few weeks, as the convoy rode at anchor in Halifax harbor, Salusbury's gentlemanly breeding made him agreeable enough as a companion, and Cornwallis spoke kindly of him in his reports to Halifax.[31] Yet as soon as the business of governing began, he found himself repeatedly bypassed by the coterie of colonials when important decisions were taken, and by Saint Valentine's Day he is sentimentally expressing in his journal the desire to return home. He was not made for the enervating job of creating a town in "hard-visaged" Nova Scotia, far from the felicities of London and vulnerable to the murderous forays of local Indians. The desire to return obsessed him until Cornwallis finally granted him leave two years later. Meanwhile, he grew cynical and vindictive. Though technically a member of council, he could not penetrate the inner circle of decision and influence. Returning to Halifax in 1752, Salusbury lasted one more winter and then gave it up for good in the summer of 1753, taking with him nothing but ugly memories of subversive

Acadians, bloodthirsty Indians, and colonial brokers. For some of his colleagues, Nova Scotia brought wealth and power without the benefit of Salusbury's connections. For Salusbury, the Nova Scotia venture was simply a prolonged interlude in an erratic and dissatisfying life.

1707–49

The lack of initiative and ambition, the sense of drift that emerges from John Salusbury's journal is characteristic of a life that had begun more auspiciously. Besides enjoying the advantages of an agreeable manner and a good education, Salusbury could claim membership in a well-established and celebrated Welsh family.[32] The European origins of the Salusburys are obscure, but the record shows that Salusburys served the Crown actively from the time of the Crusades and could claim a hint of royal blood in their veins transmitted from Katheryn of Berain, the granddaughter of an illegitimate son of Henry VII. The first Salusburys in Wales settled in the area of Llewenny with followers of the earl of Lincoln in 1283–84. At the beginning of the eighteenth century, their estate, through a series of marital arrangements, lay in the hands of Sir Robert Cotton (the Salusburys and Cottons having intermarried with some frequency), a Cheshire baronet who had established a seat at the Abbey of Combermere. The Salusburys themselves possessed Bach-y-Graig, the former estate of Sir Richard Clough, second husband of Kathryn of Berain. Here John Salusbury was born on 1 September 1707.[33] As the eldest of three surviving sons, he inherited the estate when his father, Thomas Salusbury, died in 1714,[34] leaving his wife Lucy the burden of three children and the encumbrances of heavy mortgages. Drawing on her limited means, she sent John and his brother Thomas to the Whitchurch school,[35] and from there they proceeded to Trinity Hall, Cambridge. John was admitted in 1725 and took the M.A. (*comitia regia*) in 1728. His plodding brother Thomas entered the university in 1726, apparently with a legal career in mind, but did not receive the LL.B. until 1734. He was granted an LL.D. in 1740.[36] The education of the two eldest sons (an accident incapacitated a third, Henry) exhausted the family capital, and John now found himself not only without a profession but without income from an estate heavily mortgaged and "involved in every possible Confusion & Distress"[37] at his father's death.

He set out for London to try his luck, and for a while, his daughter writes, survived as a fortune hunter and gigolo. At first, the young gallant is supposed to have fallen in with a Miss Harriott Edwards.

> She was a Young Person of large & independent Fortune, who set Reputation at Nought, & Scandal at Defiance; resolved to avoid Marriage, yet have a Son on whom to settle her Estate. She took as I have been told a fancy to my Father; whom She supplied with Money as long as her Taste to his Company subsisted, and when they parted, He picked up another female Friend, a M[rs] Stradwicke. who being divorced from her Husband led a libertine Life till all her Pelf was exhausted.[38]

For a while, he went abroad as companion to his cousin, Sir Robert Cotton, and Cotton paid all his expenses without perhaps realizing that Salusbury was corresponding with his sister, Hester, who was spurning one suitor after another in hopes of one day marrying him. Cotton came home, but Salusbury allegedly remained at Lyons for six months with "a French Marquise who died in his Arms, & left him the little he had not spent of hers before."[39] As the story goes, he returned home himself to discover that the Salusburys had borrowed money from Sir Robert to help mortgage Bach-y-Graig. As well as extending this temporary relief, Sir Robert, as lord lieutenant of the county of Denbigh, appointed John Salusbury a captain of the local militia and his deputy lieutenant in 1735.[40] But by 1738, neither Salusbury's credit nor the mortgage on the estate would bear further extension and, for the first time, the benefits of a sound marriage impressed the young squire, a marriage to his faithful cousin Hester, an heiress with a considerable estate of her own. Hester was still waiting and now promised to settle his debts if he would accept her. With some haste, Thomas Salusbury was sent to Wales early in 1739 to make a list of his brother's obligations, and when he finished in February, a marriage settlement was signed, freeing the estate of encumbrances with £1,200 of Hester's £2,500.[41] Relieved at this unexpected turn of events, Lucy Salusbury wrote Hester on 19 February to thank her for taking over the support of "poor Jack." Without it, she said, "he could not have lived."[42]

While Lucy remained alive, John was reluctant to move her from Bach-y-Graig, and he took his bride to Bodvel Hall, a seventeenth-century gatehouse in Carnarvonshire rented from Sir Thomas Hanmer.[43] Since Bodvel Hall was situated near a small estate of John Salusbury's, it was possible for Salusbury and his wife to live upon its produce, together with the proceeds of Hester's annuity. Much of John's income was dedicated to supporting his mother, who spared no expense, and his brother, who insisted on living in high style as a rising London lawyer. It was a tiresome exile for a couple accustomed to the society of cultivated friends, and it remained so until 27 January 1741, when, "after several Miscarriages from Frights, Contests Falls &c," the birth of their only child brought a brief distraction.[44] The short-tempered Salusbury did not enjoy the company of his daughter at first. "Rakish Men seldom make tender Fathers," she observed in later years, "but a Man must fondle something, and Nature pleads her own Cause powerfully when a little Art is likewise used to help it forward."[45] She consequently grew to be his favorite and, equally important, the favorite of her uncle, the childless Sir Robert Cotton, who had spurned his sister when she married the rake.

At last, Lucy Salusbury died in February 1745, leaving Bach-y-Graig completely in John's hands. She had lived so extravagantly and managed his affairs so badly that her departure only aggravated his financial difficulties.[46] No improvement lay in sight except through the support of the Cottons, and accordingly a rapprochement with Sir Robert Cotton was arranged, eased by his devotion to his niece. In the summer of 1747, the family returned to Flintshire, and the explosive John Salusbury remained civil under his brother-in-law's roof until Sir Robert suggested the time had come for him to proceed to London and seek a secure living with the assistance of John's successful brother Thomas. Move to London he did, taking his family with him, and surprisingly he achieved the break without offending the childless Sir Robert, who promised to rewrite his will in order to provide £10,000 for the child and £200 a year for his sister.[47] This was generous indeed. He also urged the family to move into his house on Albermarle Street to prepare for his arrival.

Arriving in London, John Salusbury quickly took up with his former friends, and his wife was introduced into polite society. Sir Robert sent word that he would appear in London to alter his will, but three days before his departure, he was seized with a fit of apoplexy and died. It was 27 August 1748.[48] What had seemed at first a happy solution to the family's difficulties now quickly turned to ashes, for they discovered there was no new will. Either Sir Robert had changed his mind or the will had been destroyed. Instead, the whole of his estate and his title passed into the hands of his brother, now Sir Lynch Cotton, and John Salusbury's family was as desperate as ever. Thirty years later, John's daughter, by then Mrs. Hester Thrale, remarked, "Some traces yet remain upon my mind of poor mamma's anguish and of my father's violent expressions."[49] To add to their misery, the child contracted smallpox. Shoved out of the Cotton house, they took lodgings in Lincoln's Inn Fields, abandoning for the time being their ascent into London society.

When John Salusbury received the offer of an appointment in Nova Scotia, he thus had no prospects at all. He and his family were rapidly declining into a liability for those around them, and though some encouraged him to accept, others balked at what seemed to be an ill-considered venture into the wilds of North America. Why should someone so well connected need to leave the country to survive? Edward Bridge, the steward who oversaw the running of Bach-y-Graig, wrote him,

You say in your Lre of Easter Tuesday that because you are poor I am angry with you, I wish it lay in my power to make you Rich & Happy, I blame a certain Person, whose power it was in to have saved you lately to deny you his assistance, which has surprized me very much, the Esq.ʳ when over here lately told me the affair with a great deal of Concern.[50]

The fact is that Thomas Salusbury, though well established in London, was not a wealthy man, and Sir Lynch Cotton, though he looked favorably on Hester and the child, had tired of John's feckless drifting. As the expedition was fitting out in the spring of 1749, the family got together enough cash to outfit the reluctant colonist for his voyage, but no one stepped forward to keep him home. Though he regretted leaving his wife and child with no choice but to shift from one lodging house to the other, subsisting on a pittance, his pride prevented him from turning back. He suffered the separation only as long as it took to reach Portsmouth, where he explained to Hester in the first of many forlorn letters, "not to be Able to Live up to Thy Rank without this Prostitution of That Joy Determined Me."

1749–53

If Salusbury was hoping for a quick profit, Halifax was not likely to enrich him soon. His salary of twenty shillings a day did not go far, and the funds sent by Thomas only provided a sufficient reserve for keeping up appearances. What he had, he mishandled. It was either loaned unwisely or stolen, and as he confesses in one letter, he spent too much keeping himself as a gentleman. After two years' separation from his family, without any visible improvement in his status, he wrote despondently to Hester, "All this to live thus seperated Is too much—for what—for Money. I have now declined their money employment—Knowing I will be Honest *think* it too much trouble: on that footing not worth while to have Governments Money in Keeping." The certain benefits, of course, were the generous grants offered settlers, and it seems the idea of settling did cross Salusbury's mind. In one letter, he suggests that he might start a farm. His schooner, the *Montagu*, launched in July 1750, was probably built for fishing. Dr. Crane had written the month before, "the Montagu I hope will enrich it's owner,"[51] and John Collier later kept him up to date on the fishing at Dunk Cove (now Herring Cove), where he had been granted thirty acres.[52] (This property, together with other choice holdings, was escheated when Salusbury quit the colony without making the improvements required of all settlers by the Board of Trade.)[53] Instead, with his staff of two clerks, he took up his time with the routine job of supervising the allocation and registration of lots, administering oaths to purchasers of land and performing other duties assigned him as a member of council. When the new courthouse opened, he shifted his office to a room there and made himself available for business from nine o'clock until noon, six days a week.[54]

Salusbury's appointment occupied his time, but it did not relieve his mind of his family's difficult circumstances. During the second winter, he earnestly petitioned the governor for leave to carry dispatches to England, but Cornwallis did not agree to it until August 1751. If he had waited longer, perhaps an intervention by Thomas would have brought him home anyway, since in 1751 he was negotiating a marriage and desired his brother's presence. Mrs. Thrale recalls how he had explained to her mother

that his neglect of his Brother's Affair about the Mortgage [on Bach-y-Graig] was occasioned only by his Mind being wholly taken up in this much greater Concern, that please God he should now have it in his Power to do something in return for all her Kindness, &c. &c. &c. when the first Emotions were subsided, they sate down quietly, & wrote my Father word of the approaching Felicity; desired him to get leave to come over to the Wedding, & made up their Joint Letter in an Agony of Delight. I was kissed enough, & much was hoped, & much was feared, & much was promised to be done for all of us.[55]

Clearly, John Salusbury was missed; but before he received this letter he was back in England, where "all was Gayety, Transport, & Frenzy of Enjoyment."[56] That year, Thomas married the daughter of Sir Henry Penrice, a judge of the Admiralty Courts, whom he succeeded in the judgeship with its attendant knighthood.[57] Sir Thomas Salusbury was now well fixed socially, but he would have to wait a bit longer before his wife inherited her expected fortune. Meanwhile, John Salusbury set sail for Nova Scotia again in the spring of 1752 at the urging of Lord Halifax and found the conditions in the colony even more disagreeable than before. He detested the new governor, Peregrine Hopson, and grew more irritated by the political factions scrambling for influence. It was not a comfortable place for an indifferent councillor. That winter, Sir Thomas again petitioned the Board of Trade, who expedited his brother's return by directing Hopson, "As we have reason to think, that M! Salusbury's private affairs may require his coming to England, We desire you will, upon his Application, let him have your leave for that purpose, and appoint M! Collier Register and Receiver in his Room. . . . "[58] Back in England, Salusbury had nothing to show for his three-year exile and was "gloriously out of humour"[59] when he found Sir Thomas had neglected his estate.

During the previous winter, however, Sir Henry Penrice had died, leaving the whole of his estate to his daughter, so that Sir Thomas was now able to coax money from his wife to support his poor relations in a more comfortable manner. The benefits of this marriage came none too soon. Throughout the journal and letters, John Salusbury had worried about the health of his wife and daughter, and with good reason. In his absence, Hester had attempted to live on her annuity of £125 a year, and rather than encumber the estate further, endangered her health with "her Fancy of living almost wholly on Vegetables & water."[60] She and her daughter were a pair of itinerants. In summer they were welcomed by Sir Lynch Cotton at Llewenny or by Hester's mother, Philadelphia, at East Hyde, Bedfordshire;[61] in winter they boarded on Saint Charles Street, Saint James's, and kept up their social connections. The child's education progressed at the hands of her mother.[62] But during the second sojourn in Nova Scotia, Sir Thomas's situation had improved so much that they could visit his new home, Offley Place,[63] and when John returned, Sir Thomas's marriage to the heiress of Offley enabled the judge to provide a house for them on Jermyn Street and subsequently Dean Street, Soho.

1753-62

As a companion John Salusbury was agreeable enough, and his friends found him honest and loyal, even though he could not control his affairs. In a rare tribute to his activities the first year, a lady from Halifax testifying before the Board of Trade after Davidson's dismissal told the board that he "behaves very well, and that they want a few more such, and that he takes a great deal of pains to do publick good."[64] As the Saint Paul's Church register shows, parents named their children after him. This honor was only bestowed upon prominent and respected citizens.[65] Beneath the charming exterior, however, he was a sensitive individual who sniped and carped throughout his journal and took offense at the slightest provocation. His humor seemed to consist of droll jests not always appreciated by his hearers. Thus, his affected gentility and sententiousness brought him pain, especially amid the less felicitous surroundings of Nova Scotia. His daughter recalls:

My Father was a Man of quick Parts, much Gentleman like Literature, and a Vein of humour very diverting and seemingly inexhaustible: his Conversation was showy however, not solid; few Men were ever more certain to please at Sight; but though his Talk did not consist in telling Stories, it fatigued his Hearers, who as he was not rich—made no Ceremony of letting him see it. His Sensibility—quickened by Vanity & Idleness was *keen* beyond the *Affectation* of any other Mortal, and threw him into Hypocondriack Disorders in spite of a Manly Vigorous Person, & of a Constitution eminently strong.[66]

Consequently, his journal is often indignant in tone. He resented being shoved aside; he wanted to be listened to. But instead of asserting himself as a member of council, he expressed his resentment in his journal and in letters to his wife, assigning such epithets as "King Log" to Governor Hopson, "Our Oracle" to Hugh Davidson, and "Gay's Monkey" to Benjamin Green.

During his remaining years, Salusbury prospered through the good fortune of Sir Thomas, particularly when Sir Thomas's wife died in 1759, leaving him all her money and land. In London, the family maintained a busy social schedule and entertained such friends as Dr. Crane and the family of Lord Halifax, Captain Ewer from Nova Scotia, Governor Lawrence's brother Herbert,[67] John Salusbury's intimate friend Dr. William Parker (chaplain to George III),[68] and the artist William Hogarth, a regular visitor.[69] These years might have provided a pleasant completion to an otherwise fragmented and unsatisfactory life if John Salusbury's choleric temper had not shattered the peace and quiet. The childless Sir Thomas and his wife doted on John's daughter, Hetty, who was made Sir Thomas's heiress, and when Lady Salusbury left her estate to her husband, John was overjoyed. At his request, Sir Thomas took steps to disencumber the Salusbury estate. For the first time, no serious family problems would have intruded into their lives if John Salusbury had not found a new obsession.

Hetty, an attractive and intelligent girl as well as the heiress of Offley, was being pursued by a series of earnest young men, but her father thought her far too young for this kind of intrigue. "The least mention of a Proposal to his Daughter put him in the most violent passion imaginable," wrote Mrs. Thrale in later years, and rather than arouse his ill humor, she avoided all such solicitations.[70] The protectiveness and hot temper of her father may be observed in this letter written to James Marriott around 1760 after he had intercepted Marriott's love letter:

Sir,

My daughter shewed me an extraordinary letter from you. She resents the ill-treatment as conscious that she never gave any pretence to take such liberties with Her. I think it hard that insolence and Impudence should be suffered to interrupt the tranquil state of youth and innocence.

I therefore insist on no altercations—no more trash on the subject. But should you continue to insult the poor child I do assume the Father, I shall take the Insult to myself; be then most certainly assured that I will be avenged on you, much to the detriment of your person. So help me God.

John Salusbury[71]

One suitor he could not discourage, though, was Henry Thrale, a frequent visitor to the household after Sir Thomas discovered that the London brewer's father had been born in what was now the dog kennel at Offley,[72] and in 1761 Thrale's presence hastened John Salusbury's death. That year, the two brothers accompanied Lord Halifax while he proceeded to Dublin as the new lord lieutenant of Ireland. On his return, John found two things changed: Sir Thomas was paying court to a blooming widow, a Mrs. King, and at the same time both Sir Thomas and John's own wife were plotting a marriage between Henry Thrale and Hetty.[73] When John Salusbury's ceaseless complaints and wearying exchanges with his brother made him unwelcome at Offley, he took his family and retreated to Dean Street, where Thrale pressed his suit and where the two impending marriages dominated the conversation of their acquaintants. But where joy and expectation would have followed in most families, in this one there was discord and ultimate tragedy.

In December 1762, the girl's Latin tutor, Dr. Arthur Collier, wrote her a secret note in Latin. Sir Thomas was about to marry Mrs. King, he said. He would come next day to break the news to her father. This information she concealed awkwardly, and her explosive father, suspecting a clandestine correspondence between her and Thrale, was enraged. Resolutely protecting her honesty, Hetty argued over the matter with her father until three o'clock the next morning, when she revealed the letter. Salusbury apologized and retired in an agitated frame of mind. Early the next day, he arose and left to consult Dr. Crane and his brother-in-law, Sir Lynch Cotton. The same afternoon he was carried home dead of an apoplectic stroke.[74]

There were expressions of shock and loss. Lord Halifax wrote effusively to Sir Thomas:

Nobody could be more shock'd than I was at the news of my good Friend your Brother's Death, which came suddenly on me at Dinner with my Daughters on Sunday, & poor Crane, who till then was as ignorant of the Misfortune as I was. Your Brother had been with him a long Time on the morning of the fatal Day in perfect Health & spirits, & went from him to Sir Lynch Cotton's.—our Hearts all paid, & continue to pay the Debt of Friendship & Grief on the Loss of so Worthy a Man.—I will say no more on the melancholly occassion, tho' the Love I bore your Brother might almost require it.[75]

But the family was more relieved than sorry that so joyless and purposeless a life had ended.[76] Free of her father's petty jealousies, Hetty married Thrale, the Southwark brewer, the following October[77] and later distinguished herself as an author, particularly for the biography of her intimate friend Dr. Samuel Johnson. Her mother, a cheerful and spirited woman despite a life of upheaval and disappointment, remained partially dependent on Sir Thomas until her death in 1773.[78]

When John Salusbury died, his experiences in Nova Scotia became a part of family legend, and the Nova Scotia connection receded into the background until 1785, when Hetty, by now the wife of the Italian singer Gabriel Piozzi, examined her father's papers and discovered extensive land grants in

Halifax that promised to be extremely valuable. Obsessed with the idea of regaining her father's property, she engaged a Halifax lawyer to take her case to a Halifax court but learned after several years of investigation that they had been taken by the escheator.[79] Among the rest of his papers, though, there were seven small notebooks and a handful of letters recording these unusual experiences in a fragmented and elliptical way and, like the journalist in *Spectator* No. 317, "taking so much care of a Life that was filled with such inconsiderable Actions, and received so very small Improvements."[80] As a salaried official yet a virtual outsider, Salusbury had described the early years in Halifax from an unusual point of view. Many of his comments were personal, but others referred to conditions, events, and individuals directly affecting the settlement's progress.[81]

The Indian Threat

According to John Salusbury, two of Governor Cornwallis's first objectives were to secure the allegiance of the Acadian deputies and to sign a peace with the Micmacs. Though Cornwallis failed to accomplish the first, he did get the Indians to sign a treaty. Peace did not inevitably follow, however, for as soon as the chiefs withdrew to the woods, the settlement virtually returned to a state of siege when the French brought their naval and military forces into play to strangle it. In support of the French interest, local Indians attacked travelers, raided towns and terrified families whenever they wished. In response Cornwallis called on three regular British regiments: the fortieth (Phillips's/Hopson's, stationed there for forty years), the forty-fifth (Warburton's, one of two regiments sent to Louisbourg in 1746) and the forty-seventh (Lascelles's, dispatched from Ireland in 1750). These soldiers were drilled in conventional European tactics. The Indians' stealth and knowledge of the terrain frustrated their orthodox methods and even thwarted the independent companies of rangers Cornwallis recruited in New England. In all

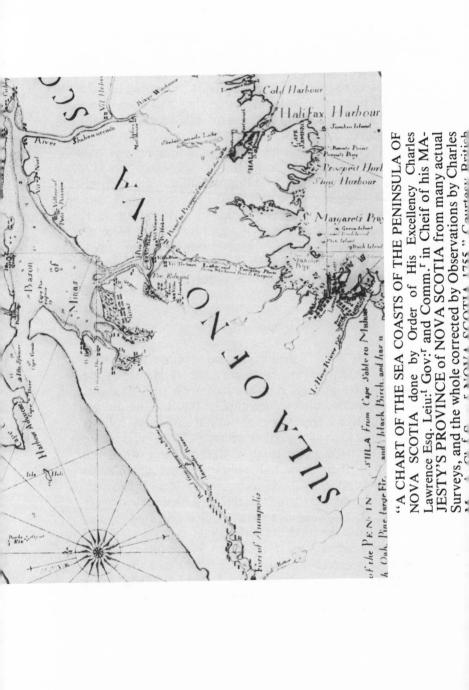

"A CHART OF THE SEA COASTS OF THE PENINSULA OF NOVA SCOTIA done by Order of His Excellency Charles Lawrence Esq. Leiu.t Gov.r and Comm.r in Chief of his MA-JESTY'S PROVINCE of NOVA SCOTIA from many actual Surveys, and the whole corrected by Observations by Charles

the skirmishes, complained one observer, "some of the regulars have been pillaged of their scalps;—but never have they been able to produce a single trophy of that kind, to the enemy's loss."[82] On their own ground, the settlers found the Indians' strange garb and manners diverting. During the treaty ceremonies of 1749, one patronizing gentleman compared the Indians to the Hottentots:

> they are in manners and dress not inferior to them; their faces are rubbed over with vermillion, and a-cross their nose and forehead are regularly drawn black lines, to beautify themselves the more: Their ears are bored full of holes, and adorned with tobacco pipes, and ribbons of different colours; their cloaths are of the right homespun-grey, but intolerably ragged: The *French* supply them with those articles: Their squaws or women dress equally as gay as the men.[83]

Outside their sphere of influence, however, such a strange spectacle threw settlers into a panic so that between Cornwallis's first treaty (essentially a renewal of the 1725 treaty)[84] and the one reported by Salusbury in 1752 (an offer of more material benefits and the opportunity to trade) the Micmacs persisted.

To complicate Cornwallis's task, the Micmacs were not united as a nation. Each local band acted independently towards the British and required different treatment. While the Saint John River Indians might behave in a friendly and peaceable manner, those at Canso, Halifax, or Chignecto would be committing artrocities like the ones observed during the three attacks on the vulnerable sawmill run by Major Gilman at Dartmouth. These attacks made Salusbury uneasy. On 30 September 1749, a party of Indians killed four of Gilman's workers, scalped two and decapitated the other two.[85] On 26 March 1751, again they attacked the sawmill, killing soldiers and settlers alike and sparing neither women nor children. "A little baby was found lying by its father and mother," wrote a settler, "all three scalped. The whole town was a scene of butchery, some having their hands cut off, some their bellies ripp'd open, and others their brains dash'd out.''[86] A much larger raiding party returned on 13 May and ruined the hamlet by pulling down houses and destroying property, undeterred by the extra troops sent across the harbor by Cornwallis. This time, they killed a sergeant who ran from his bed to assist, "and not being content with his life, cut his left arm off, and afterwards scalp'd him."[87] About fourteen prisoners were taken. Outraged by this open treachery, Cornwallis attempted to take the intitiative in 1750 by engaging Sylvanus Cobb to hunt the alleged instigator, the French missionary Abbé Le Loutre. He was to sail to Boston to raise 100 men, proceed into the Basin of Chignecto, and surprise as many Indians and settlers as he could so as to take them hostage. For every Indian scalp, he was to be paid £10 — £50 for Le Loutre's.[88] But Cobb found recruits scarce in Boston, and when he revealed the plan by advertising for them, Cornwallis cancelled the operation. Throughout Salusbury's journal, no further progress is reported.

The Chignecto Expedition of 1750 and the Role of Naval Forces in Nova Scotia

John Salusbury's account of how he accompanied Charles Lawrence as an observer on the Chignecto expedition of April 1750 is one of the more interesting features of his journal. More than any diary previously published, it describes in detail how a detachment of about 400 men under Lawrence's command marched from Halifax to Minas and proceeded by ship to attempt a landing on the shores of Chignecto Basin, where they were to erect a blockhouse in sight of the French commander, Pierre La Corne. As part of his mission to establish the British presence in various parts of Acadia, Cornwallis picked out this spot because it was situated on the Missiguash River, a de facto boundary accepted by both British and French. (It is now part of the New Brunswick-Nova Scotia border.) This meant the blockhouse would have to be constructed on the British side of Beaubassin rather than on the

French-held Beauséjour ridge, from where the French and their Indian allies controlled the area west of the isthmus.

Lawrence's force, with Captain Francis Bartelo as second in command, was taken to Fort Sackville at the head of Bedford Basin on 5 April and began the six-day march to Minas to rendezvous with their transports. Arriving on 11 April, they sat nervously for a week awaiting the arrival of Captain John Rous in the *Albany*, each day affording the Acadians a better chance to leak their intentions to the enemy and wipe out all chance of surprise. When the *Albany* finally did arrive with her three armed sloops and a schooner in consort, she did not set sail from Minas until 18 April,[89] so that Lawrence did not get his troops ashore until four days later. Even so, the British boats made the mistake of landing on the Beauséjour side. La Corne confronted Lawrence and ordered him to leave, but as Lawrence prepared to cross the river to the village of Chignecto (on the British side) La Corne and Abbé Le Loutre ordered it evacuated and set alight, and he arrived to see a once prosperous settlement in ashes. Finding himself heavily outnumbered by the collection of "French Troops, Canadeans, Rebel Inhabitants and the Savages"[90] and lacking protection from the stormy weather, he prudently withdrew. That same day, the convoy wound its way out the basin again, arriving back in Minas on the twenty-sixth with nothing to show for the operation.[91]

But that was not the end of the matter. As Salusbury mentions himself, Lawrence returned on 4 September with a much stronger force and the equipment required to build a palisaded fort. (Salusbury had lost his courage the first time round and did not accompany him.) This time, he carefully landed on the British side, and again a French and Indian force turned back his landing party. It was still early in the morning, and they had made no progress. Finally, at 10 A.M., Lawrence decided to lead an assault himself, and he made short work of it. "I observed the fireing to Slacken on Chignecto side," wrote Rous in the *Albany* log, "& our Troops advancing with fixed Bayonnets drove the Savages out of the Dykes, with the Loss on our side of 5 men Killed &

a few wounded, the Troops at Noon makeing the Necessary preparations for a Lodgment onshore.''[92] Fort Lawrence was ready for occupation by October, and Lawrence, who kept in touch with Salusbury all the while, remained in command until the following summer. (Salusbury awaited his return before sailing for England.) Meanwhile, the Marquis de la Jonquière, governor of Canada, countered with two forts of his own straddling the Isthmus of Chignecto: Fort Gaspereau, an outpost on the northern side, and Fort Beauséjour, just over a mile south of Fort Lawrence. This was the status quo when Lieutenant–Colonel Robert Monckton took command of Fort Lawrence in August 1752, and thus it remained until he captured Beauséjour in the summer of 1755.

Clearly, from 1749 to 1755, naval forces contributed to the success achieved at outposts such as Chignecto even though Halifax was not yet a major naval port and the Admiralty was not taking a direct hand in the territorial maneuverings in Acadia. The Admiralty did assign a station ship (Rous's sloop *Albany*) to Nova Scotia in 1749, and when the French began to press the following year, they sent two more sloops, *Trial* and *Hound*, commanded by Edward Le Cras and Thomas Dove. Otherwise, Cornwallis took the direction of coastal patrols into his own hands.[93] His ad hoc arrangements were not revealed to Salusbury at first, and in June 1750 he comments sarcastically, ''I am let into no State Secrets, and bussiness seemingly industriously Kept from Me.'' Though he faithfully records the comings and goings of armed vessels, he does not seem to understand that a rather unusual ''sea militia'' composed of local ships and captains also operated in the area to keep open the lines of communication between Halifax, Annapolis, and Chignecto.[94] When the schooners *Anson* and *Warren*, ships hired out to the Admiralty by John Gorham, received their discharge, Cornwallis promptly hired them back with funds provided for the colony's defense. With these, he supplemented the three armed vessels *Ulysses, New Casco,* and *Dove* inherited from Louisbourg. Outnumbered by the superior French naval presence in Nova Scotia waters, they limited themselves to supplying existing settlements and after 1752 left the French free to maintain their routes between Louisbourg and Acadia via the Northumberland Strait.

The Money Crisis of 1750

The shortage of currency in Halifax preoccupies Salusbury throughout these papers. As early as November 1749, he writes, "Our treasury is shut up and no Money to be had." In August 1752, he explains to his wife that he is drawing bills on his brother Thomas because "Our treasury Here is so poor that it would be almost a shame to draw on it." In the intervening months, he heaps strong criticism on those responsible for the weakening financial condition of the colony as day after day he sits through council meetings seeking solutions but foreseeing no improvement.

Unlike many other North American settlements, Halifax did not spring into being as a mercantile venture but as part of a scheme to settle Nova Scotia with Protestants. There was no balance of trade at first. What nature did not yield up the settlers imported, and with nothing to export, they paid for these items with cash. Cornwallis first realized his precarious financial state in October 1749 when he exhausted the supply of coin he had brought with him. If he did not contrive new ways of procuring provisions, supplies, and building materials, he reckoned, the settlers would not survive the first winter. Fortunately, Cornwallis was able to turn to Boston. Boston merchants had already financed the Annapolis garrison with funds sent from London, using bills of exchange that the governor drew on various departments. These bills were exchanged in Boston for New England currency and then remitted from Boston to London for British goods. Using this method, Cornwallis obtained money and supplies until 1752. After that, money was sent directly from London, though by then the colony was capable of negotiating its own bills of exchange and encouraging exports.[95]

In the meantime, Cornwallis kept Halifax afloat as best he

could.[96] For extra funds, he was authorized to draw on the London merchant Chauncey Townshend, a British government agent, through Townshend's agent Christopher Kilby. But Townshend, it seems, dishonored bills and refused payment, and Kilby gave priority to his own personal bills. Now Cornwallis turned to less orthodox methods. Distrusting the Boston merchants, he dispatched his own representative, Lieutenant William Martin, to negotiate for stores and dollars, and Martin carried out these duties in Boston from October 1749 to July 1750.[97] Cornwallis thereby obtained better rates, for Martin successfully exchanged small bills wherever he could. Whenever dollars were in short supply, he turned for credit first to the firm of Apthorp and Hancock and then to DeLancy and Watts.[98] But again, because Cornwallis had spent so much, his bills were not honored in London. Nova Scotia's credit vanished. No more bills could be sold. Apthorp and Hancock offered to relieve Cornwallis in return for a monopoly on the colony's business. Cornwallis refused. He was growing more desperate, and workmen building the town were clamoring for their pay. At this point, Salusbury reports the departure of Secretary Hugh Davidson on 25 May 1750 to negotiate in Boston. Though Apthorp and Hancock were already due thousands of pounds, they finally agreed to a loan of £3,000 if Cornwallis would agree to their terms in the future, and Cornwallis was barely saved from their excessive demands when Parliament voted him emergency grants.

From their offices in London, the Board of Trade watched these events closely, satisfied that Cornwallis was doing his best with the available resources. They did not become concerned until the spring of 1750 after interviewing returning Halifax settlers who testified that Davidson was trading with public funds and converting public stores, especially rum and molasses, to his own profit. His accomplices, they said, all seemed to be his fellow Scots, men who had arrived in the colony penniless and had joined the prosperous without difficulty. So many people believed Davidson was trading illegally, a Halifax woman testifed in May 1750, that they had proposed drawing up a petition but were afraid.[99] (From November 1749, Salusbury suspects Davidson's activities and directs some of his most scathing comments against him.) The records show that while he was in Boston, Martin purchased for himself and Davidson the sloop *Cornwallis* and that the two rented it to the colony for £500 a month for conveying stores to Halifax.[100] Davidson had displeased the board in March 1750 when he ordered a supply of medicines for the Halifax hospital from Richard Oswald & Company without authority.[101] While he was in Boston preoccupied with the money crisis, they started to inquire further,[102] and when they confronted him with their suspicions, Davidson wrote to Viscount Dupplin, a member of the board,

> I may have committed Errors, I may have often failed in Forms, being neither bred in public Offices nor indeed to business—but Your Lordships shall never find that I fail to do the duty of my Office with fidelity & honour.[103]

Cornwallis defended Davidson's integrity too, though he assured the board "I shall take care that neither he, or any Person in Publick Employm! be Concern'd in Trade for the future."[104] As a further precaution, he established in July a committee composed of Salusbury, Green, and William Steele to look into the allegations, and Davidson responded by writing the board a long memorial protesting his innocence.[105] Unmoved by this appeal, they recalled him in September to put his case in person. As soon as he had gone, the Halifax populace apparently found their voices. "Now the fellow is tumbling," Salusbury wrote to his wife, "All our people Cry out against Him." By December he was summoned before the board, and the principal witness was Sir Danvers Osborn, formerly a member of Cornwallis's council and a brother-in-law of Lord Halifax. Sir Danvers introduced evidence of accounting irregularities uncovered by the Halifax committee and repeated Cornwallis's decision never to trust Davidson with public funds if he returned.[106] In his defense, Davidson explained some of the irregularities satisfactorily, but he could not convince the board of his innocence. Concluding their hearings in July 1751, they pronounced Davidson unfit for the position of secretary.[107] He had hampered and embarrassed Cornwallis at a critical moment and would not return to public service in Nova Scotia again.

That same year, council turned its attention to making the colony self-supporting, and though Salusbury reports its decisions, he provides no explanation. It first adopted a bounty system to encourage agriculture and fishing, a system funded from the proceeds of an excise of 6*d*. per gallon on rum and other retailed spirits. (This was the first money raised independently in Nova Scotia without the help of the British government.) Next, it placed an impost of 3*d*. on all imported liquor to encourage a local distilling industry and, because this would cause molasses to be imported from the West Indies, to stimulate trade. At the same time, it paid a bounty of 10*s*. per ton to builders with a view to starting a local shipbuilding industry and providing local ships for the anticipated increase in trade. Throughout 1752 and 1753, trade and commerce expanded dramatically in Halifax, and an identifiable mercantile class emerged. This coterie of merchants formed the first political lobby in the town, and before John Salusbury returned to England in 1753, it had already started to assert its influence on public policy.

The Merchants' "Party"

Next to Hugh Davidson and Benjamin Green, Salusbury most frequently attacks Joshua Mauger, a merchant who traded with the French and encouraged popular resistance to council. As victualler to the Navy, he profited from Cornwallis's precarious financial state and used his position to extend his mercantile empire. Salusbury refers obliquely throughout the journal to the many enterprises in New England and Nova Scotia that brought him into contact with the enemy and seems to suspect Mauger of being a fifth columnist not to be trusted. There is no evidence of Mauger's disloyalty, however, and Salusbury's effusions are probably a reaction to Mauger's repeated confrontations with council.

Mauger was a Jerseyman, and he spent the first few years of his career as a ship's master. The details of his early life, however, are scant. By 1749, at the age of twenty-four, he had moved himself into the position of victualler to the Royal Navy at Louisbourg, and when the British evacuated the fortress, moved his operation to Halifax, where he remained until 1760. At first he attempted to continue trading with Louisbourg until Cornwallis forbade all trade with the French. From that point, Cornwallis constantly suspected him of smuggling but could not convict him. He even tried to dismiss him as victualler to the Navy but was promptly informed by the Board of Trade that no law or treaty prohibited trading with Louisbourg. In 1751, Mauger erected a distillery on the outskirts of Halifax (taking advantage of the threepenny-a-gallon duty on rum) and built up a lucrative business in Halifax and such outposts as Chignecto and Piziquid. He also acquired considerable parcels of land in the Halifax area, including a beach on Cornwallis (now McNab's) Island that bears his name to this day, and he owned over twenty vessels. This made him the most powerful trader in Halifax.[108] By means of his wealth and his influence over the lesser Halifax merchants, mostly New England men, he constantly bothered Governors Cornwallis, Hopson, and Lawrence, especially because his trading network kept him in touch with the French and his connections in London provided an outlet for his complaints. There are numerous instances of his interference in council business, but the one that preoccupies Salusbury towards the end of his journal is the "justices' affair," the most absorbing event in Halifax for several months in 1753 and an early instance of the merchant faction's activities.

From the beginning of the settlement, New England and British settlers were sharply divided. When Salusbury returned from England in July 1752, he also noticed that the people were "forming foolish little divisions among themselves" in a more deliberate way. By December, the polarization was evident when a charge was laid against Ephraim Cooke, a former commander of the transport *Baltimore* who had settled in the town. Cooke opposed the justices of the Inferior Court of Common Pleas and claimed the support of the populace. He himself had been commissioned a justice of the court and, like all the other justices, had been given a separate commission.[109] Later, Cornwallis had issued a general commission including Cooke, and Cooke continued to sit on the bench until a dissatisfied Cornwallis dismissed him. This time he issued another commission with Cooke's name left out. Acting on the supposed authority of the original, separate commission, Cooke now issued a warrant for an arrest, and as a result he was tried and fined £5. Cooke behaved "with great insolence" towards the court. The court responded by sending him to jail. On his release the next day, they further fined him £20 and ordered him to give a security of £500 for his good behavior for a year. While still at liberty, the stubborn Cooke again persisted in his claim and was indicted again, but this time a jury acquitted him. Insulted, the judges applied for an inquiry. At the same time, a group of settlers set to work to discredit them, splitting the town throughout the winter of 1753 as the hearings continued. Unless the matter were handled deftly, Hopson feared, it could destroy the society nursed along through the difficulties of the first three years.

The justices were Charles Morris, John Duport, James Monk, Joseph Scott, and William Bourne. At the council meeting on 3 January 1753, council heard a lengthy memorial signed by forty-seven "Merchants Traders and principal Inhabitants of the Town of Hallifax" (including Mauger, Nesbitt, Zouberbuhler, Magee, and Clapham) accusing the justices of partiality and other misdemeanors. Specifically, they declared the justices had acted partially by denying Cooke the best opportunity for a defense and rejecting the validity of the original license granted him by Cornwallis. On 9 January, they also heard a memorial from merchants and other settlers acting on the justices' behalf and a reply from the justices themselves.[110] After hearing evidence almost daily until 19 February, council reviewed the complaints and then rejected them outright. In particular, they found the complaint of Ephraim Cooke insupportable, though they feared their decision would deepen the divisions already prevalent in the town.

The whole affair concluded on 1 March when council made its final statement. Though Salusbury says Acting Secretary Cotterell wrote the speech, Lawrence was asked to deliver it, perhaps in the hope that his reputation as an officer and his popularity would make it more acceptable. (Salusbury did not think Lawrence was aware of this.) Some of the parties involved, it noted, had acted in the best interests of the colony, but others had not. Then it went on to say,

> It is not without concern that we see also, among the Complainants, some of a Very different sort, Some whom we can scarcely suppose to have been able to have formed the least Judgement of the matter lately exhibited, Some who have scarce any connection with this Place and some Others who we cannot but think would have been more properly employ'd in the pursuit of their own occupations, and as we can never suppose that the latter became concerned through the Influence of the former, we fear it is too much occasioned by an inattention to their Own affairs a thing so fatally prevalent in this Town and which never fails to be the Source of much publick disturbance, much private Calamity.[111]

Observing the great loss of time and productivity resulting from a relatively unimportant matter, council directed that in the future, persons seeking redress were to lay their cases before council itself. With an air of benevolence, the speech ended with these words:

> We cannot conclude without earnestly recommending Peace and Unanimity to all, a thing so necessary at all times for the general good, but more especially at this Time and in this Place where his Majestv's Government is

allready too much obstructed by the Malice and wicked designs of his Secret Enemys, that possibly may be round about us.[112]

Mauger's "party" had failed to undermine the authority of the justices, and Mauger himself, Salusbury thought, had failed to "Bully Himself into the Council." While council now turned to more important matters, the experience revealed to Hopson council's inability to deal with the more complicated legal questions. He therefore recommended to the Board of Trade the appointment of a chief justice and an attorney-general.

Expeditions of Honour

Book 1[1]

[12 July to 3 October 1749]

Wensday 12th July. The Governor swore into office before the Council held on board the Canning Frigate.[2] I attend'd Him. Hot and Clear.

Thursday 13th. Hot and Clear. Gates order'd to the Harbors Mouth after a schooner suppos'd lurking to take off some of our people—we brought four Deserts from Point pleasant, and they were mitily treated.

Friday 14th. Hot and Clear. the new Council swore In on board the beaufort—where the Governor takes His Quarters. The Deputies from Menis [Minas] Attend. the declaration and Oath read to them—the Oath they object to—their Answer expected in a fortnight.[3] Cicane between the french and the Indians. a little menagement with Our force will bring 'em to reason.

Saturday 15th. Hot and Clear. Attend C[ouncil]. at ten at night Cooloy[4] brought advice that the Indians assemble in Great Numbers at St Johns—this is scare to be reconcil'd with the Peace M[r] Shirley[5] is treating with them. Rouse I Hope will give a Good Account of their settlement at S[t] Johns.[6] Numbers of sloops come in dayly. the work goes on very well.

Sunday 16th. hard rain in the Morn: clear'd up and fine weather in the Even.

Monday 17th. Hot and Clear. loundg'd on shore after Council.

Tuesday 18th. Swore in Justices.[7] an Order for Constables.[8] Hot and Clear. went to the beach with [Charles ?].

Wensday 19th. Clear and Warm with a breeze, an English shower at two. the Constables swore in with the proper solemnity. the settlers much pleas'd with an Election.

Thursday 20th. Hot and Clear. Loundg'd all Day fishing with Lloyd[9]—with Leave &c——

Hear of Commissions &c. nothing said.[10] very hard.
A Guinea to Rumball.[11]
Driv out—as little in the way as possible—[12]

Friday 21st. rain with fogg—

Saturday 22nd. Hot and Clear.

Sunday 23d. Hot and Clear. a sermon on shore. walk'd to point pleasant. a schooner from Lewisburg—Coll Hopson expected.

Not a word—at a loss to think. Wrote L[ord] H[alifax] Tom[13] Hett[y].[14]

Monday 24th. Hot and Clear. The Diamond a french ship taken up for a transport by Hopson with troops from Lewisburg arriv'd at 10 at night.

Tuesday 25th —three more french ships came in with the Garisson from Lewisburg—Mr Hopson out in the Offin[g]. Warm and Clear in the Morn: with the strongest breeze we have had Here —heavy rain falls at night. the Everly sails for England.

Wensday—26th. the rain continues almost all night—Warm and Clear. Mr Hopson Arrives with the Garison from Lewisbourg in five french ships—Our Own returning with Him with baggage &c. I bath'd at the point.

Thursday 27th—Blustering with rain and with a fog—neither cold for the season nor the Climate but different from any Day I have seen Here. Dine and sup aboard. Coll Hopson with the Governor. Swore of the Council &c[15]—Morgans wife adjudg'd.[16]

Friday 28th. the wind still Higher at SSW yet Clear and not so warm as yesterday. Council swore in. Din'd aboard Sphinx &c—better be out of the way than in anyone's &c &c.[17]

Not a word——as usual &c&—

Saturday 29th—Clear but not so warm with a brisk wind. on board the Beaufort.

Sunday 30th July—Clear and warm. the Deputies from Menis Arriv'd. a sloop and schooner from Boston with Gorhams Brother.[18]

Monday 31st July—Clear and warm. Morn and Even. Calm midday. a breeze—Cooler these last four days than usual. The Deputies attend'd to day. their answer to be return'd tomorrow—easyly got over the Article of religion—nothing suppos'd as in England. not to bring Arms—Nothing either in point of Danger. Nothing objected Even by them as to the Oath. therefore if heartily Good Subjects and they have their properties [be]hind them and we can protect them it must do.[19] the Colliery granted—and the Copper—by Our Oracle.[20]

walk'd the Even on shore. Supp'd and din'd—dumb as usual.

to Rumbal
A Guinea

Tuesday August the first—the Deputies Answers given. Religion granted. to behave as Good subjects insisted on and the Oath without reserve—the 15th of October the last day, or to quit the Province. too long a Day perhaps in our Climate—as they may expect more last words—with our forces and Right certainly most easyly menag'd. How Councils may turn out think not of—the Work upon— Well and English are well enough if well us'd—Where is the [25mm.] fairly on point of Labor or Industry in any people more—if treated to their Humor—Clear and Warm.

Tuesday August 1st.
the Governor Din'd on board Mr Hopson—No notice taken &c

"A PLAN of Chebucto Harbour. With the Town of Hallefax by Moses Harris Surveyor 1749." Courtesy British Library.

Explanation

A. Harbour Mouth	N. Bing's Beach
B. Red Island	O. America Point
C. Deadman's Beach	P. Stags Point
D. Scarborough Cove	Q. Bays Mouth
E. Wattering Plat	R. Torrington's Bay
F. Gull Point	S. Summer Cove
G. Spaniards Shoal	T. Winter Cove
H. Pleasant Point	U. Town of Hallifax
I. Hawks River	W. Warburtons Camp
K. Georges Island	X. Warrens Point
L. Lobster's Hole	Y. Gorhams Point
M. Little Beach	Z. Rowses Island

Our Hero[21]—said that the Good Old Queen appear'd in Her Grotto at Richmond—and that the King had Kick'd Her Guts out &c &c— and this stuff constantly—[22] a breeze at 11 till six or it would be too Hot Even at sea—Calm night and Morn: but in the woods this breeze takes not place.

Wensday 2^d. Clear and Warm—Din'd with Davids[23]—Enquir'd for at supper—I care not. Ships dayly from Lewisbourg new England &c. the Deputies went Homewards this Morn: building the Governor House on shore.

Thursday 3^d. Warm and Clear in the Bason and on shore—I went into the Bason with Gates. but a flying fog where the Beaufort rides.

3^d. a Council of War[24]——what now.

Friday August 4th. Hot and Clear except a flying fog at noon where the ships ride—Brewse laying out the town;[25] Ewer[26] taken in[27]—Mr Hopson preparing for His departure. Our Oracle Din'd with Him—All the better—it is not possible He can be long lik'd by men of sense—[33mm.] Cooloy the fawning flatterer—impertinent f—l—Gr[eat] Liberties. that's the way Out.

Mem: New England Men and schooners.
Labradour[28] [42mm.]—against the World.

August Saturday 5th. Warm and Clear—rain at five—Order'd to make out lots for the division of the town.

Sunday August 6—Rain in Morning but without fog—a fine Clear afternoon and warm as usual—Order'd to prepare for drawing the Lots.

Strange way of speaking—Mind it not. Duty shall be done—refreshing showers and seasonable had we Grain or Grass in Question. Hardly spoke to in the Affair— Dumb on both sides as Aforsd.

Monday August 7th.—this day the Diamond saild. recd my Commission for Register. Clear and Warm.

Tuesday 8th August. Clear and Warm. Attend'd in drawing the Lots and Registring them. Ships come in constantly from Lewisbourg with Ordinance stores—this Lewisbourg affair tho' it supplies us in some measure gives much trouble to the Governor.

Wednesday 9th. finish'd drawing the Lots—the people seem satisfy'd—every one their share fairly. ten Lots remain—Waited on the Governor to shew Him the Minutes of the Register with Collier—Din'd on board the Sphinx. danc'd and sprain'd my Leg—lay that night on board the Sphinx.

> One Guinea to Collier.
> Not word when the Minutes were shown nor Word about Collier.
> At a Loss to Guess how this Affair will turn out.

Thursday 10th. Went with Davids tho' Lame a fishing. took plenty of Mackarel.

Friday 11th. Keep my Cabin Lame. blows harder and colder than Usual with heavy rain.

Saturday 12th. Keeping Cabin lame. Hot and Clear.

Sunday 13th. Lame in my Cabin. warm & Clear. the St. Johns Indians arrive with Capn Howe.

Monday 14th. Agree to a Peace on the same terms as the last at Annapolis or rather ratify that. Attend Council still Lame.

> [14?]–The Ulisses gone to Boston with Davids—the Artilary with Capn Martin[29] gone on a trade for some body [20mm.] Right.

Tuesday 15th—the Indians sign the Peace—in Council Still lame—warm—with rain.

> 15—the Indians propos'd a Defensive Alliance. not ap-

prov'd of by Hopson—I wish it had. *His reasons on that subject not conclusive to Me.

Wensday 16. Warm and Clear—still lame. write to my Lord.

Thursday 17th. lame but crawl About—fine weather.

17—Howe went away with His Indians by Water[30]—three travell'd Over land—for fear of Accidents and to prevent their being surpris'd.

Friday 18th. fine weather. still lame. Gorham complains of an insult from the Indians. they took their Arms and fird over the Heads of His people[31]—Gates sent to the bottom of the Bay to enquire into the Affair—found One Indian who told Him they were drunk—but gone Cobagate[32] to their Priest.[33] 7 Only took the Arms. in all 40.

[1]8th. Scot[34] sail'd. Good luck Attend Him. Coll Mascarene also for Annapolis.
Still in the same Hole in Every Respect.

Saturday 19th. Clear and warm. wrote to L. C. Tom.[35] sent by C[ornwallis?]. sorry I spoke to Goose as still Lame—Din'd on board the Sphinx.

The French uneasy at the order.
Indians some better menagement necessary.
Scot succedes. if not &c &c.
Scottmen & fair Lady Arriv'd from Boston.
Mem—next time no Private Friendships when Absent Alone.

Sunday. Clear and Warm. 20th August. Still the fogs hang out at sea. Lame.

Mem: Sunday 20th. to Rumball one Guinea and Half to pay the Washer woman to be Accounted for.

Monday 21st. Clear and Warm. Coll Hopson intends to sail in the Brotherhood. Coll Hopson sail'd about two—with the Alexander [and] Merry Jack for England. the London intend'd but stopp'd—I am sorry for that—the Wilmington and Wincelsea for Ireland. All the Indians withdrawn since Gorhams affair—It is supposed to be to consult with their Priest at Cobagate. No Good to us can be the result of such a Meeting.

Monday 21st. Rumball accounted for the money.

Tuesday 22d. down in the Basin with Lloyd[36] to Heave up a vessel—it will be done—She lies in a pretty Cove. Warm and Clear with a refreshing shower. Better of my Lameness.

Wensday 23d August. Warm and Clear. An Alarm about the Indians. Have taken some our people about Canso[37]—Gorhams Brother[38] order'd to Bay Vert. met this news at sea and return'd for Orders. the News true the french Keep the Hay for Lewisbourg—but How can they answer all this?

23d. nothing well will be done without Mailiard—and I do not expect it and I can tell why.

Thursday 24th August. Rain but warm at seven Morn: Continues all Day. On shore with Collier about Registring &c. wet. came on board to dine. better of my Lameness.
This night an Alarm in the Camp. the soldiers tolerably Alert. the Generality of the settlers behave steady and well.

24. Rouse Arriv'd.

Friday 25th. Clear but sultry—thunder at five in the Afternoon. more violent than any I have heard Here—tho' not so strong as I have heard Often in England. Gorhams Brother gone to enquire into the Canso affair.

25. take it &c &c &c—not to be told the trick, when pro-

pos'd &c—by J. L.[39] The same in the Whole—foolish ensign—Clappams people taken at Canso.

Saturday 26. Clear but colder than usual. din'd with little[40] with leave—a poor fellow stabed by a Swiss.

26. a person stab'd on shore—the Crimenal taken.[41]

Sunday 27th. Clear. rather Cool. sultry in the Evening.

Monday 28th. Clear and Warm Morn and Even: somewhat Cool and refreshing. A Council Held to consider of the tryal of the Murderer. this is the fourth stabing Affair since we came Here but none fatal till Now.

Tuesday 29th—Went to the Sphinx. Lloyd[42] return'd from His Cruise. Anwyl overset in His boat. two persons lost. Warm and Clear.

Wensday 30th. Warm and Clear. the Liverpool ship with Settlers arriv'd: 118—trouble to put them in any possesion as the lots in town are full.

Thursday 31st August—Clear Warm at Midday—somewhat cool in the Morn and Even——A very solemn tryal of the Person that stab'd the Sailor—and convicted by a Jury.[43]

31st. Scot return'd. I wish He had succeed'd better. did all He could. Mailard gone to St. John's Isle.[44] the Indians Assembl'd there—not for our Good. they may teaze but not Essentially Hurt the settlement. If they should the S[t] John's River Indians would be of Use now—had their proposal been attend'd to.

Friday Sep[r] the first 1749. my birth day. one and forty. Does Hetty think of Me. Grant me O God a Happy Year. Clear and Warm. sat on A Rock by the sea side most part of the Day Alone. thank God for My Health and Grant me O God the Continuance of it. neither din'd nor sup'd on board. at Lutterels[45] at Dinner. call'd at Cooks.[46] Even the Governor not well.[47] Hetty surely thinks of Me this Day—God bless

Her and the little Girl. Tom is in a Crowd, He thinks not of me. God bless Him and poor Harry.[48]

Saturday 2^d Sepr the poor fellow executed.[49] Clear. the prisoners taken at Canso return'd to Our Governor by the french Commander at Lewisbourg with Compliments &c. that He approv'd not of the conduct of the Indians, but that the Indians plead'd that Our people Ow'd them a hundr'd pounds—and this was done to secure that Money—the Deputies from Menis came again—On the Old Story.

Sunday 3^d Sepr Clear but Cool. at night rain.

3^d. by a Messenger from Annapolis the Detachment order'd for Menis had not March'd

Monday 4th Sepr. Heavy rain continues with wind but no[t] so Cool as yesterday. the storm rises and blows very hard at NE. expected a Council today to hear what the French Deputies have to say.

Tuesday 5th Sepr. The Storm of wind still continues so that the Council can not Meet today on the Affair of the Deputies—as it is unsafe to come on board from the shore. Cool to day—it is only what I expected the Autumnal Equinoctial Storm.

Wensday 6. A long conference with the Deputies—they sent a Memorial sign'd by a thousand French as I thought somewhat insolent &c. the Governor Answer'd it—Still refused taking the Oath—still pretend their fear of the Indians. Argued with but to no purpose—why All this?

6. I guess right I beleive.

thursday 7th. clear and very Warm at Midday. a small hoar [hoarfrost] in the Mornings.

Friday 8th. clear and As yesterday. Moreau sent to Menis and Gorham to the Head of the Bay. and [Russell?] gone to the Mowers.

Saturday 9th. the weather as before—

Sunday 10th. the weather As before. the Neptune arriv'd last from Cork, with Letters from Hetty to Me and One from Crane.

10th. Gates sent to Gorham at the Bottom of the Bay. not a word from Tom.

Monday 11th. still fine weather. the Governor din'd on board Rouse. write to Crane Sr Lynch[50] and Hetty—a ball on board the Sphinx.

11. Poor pill[51] slighted—a fig for that.

Tuesday 12th. went down to Gorhams encampment at the Cod[52] of the Bay. it will answer the End—the Governor there. the weather as before—the London sailed.

Pill still nobody.

Wensday 13th—the weather as before. the Ulisses return'd—with several sloops and schooners from Newengland and Else where with Lumber Whores and Artificers &c &c—the Governor dind with Little.

On Board the Sphinx with [Filby?].

Thursday 14th. the weather continues the same—I Din'd at littles. the Governor there.

Friday 15. on board—the wind at S West. the Albany and fair Lady in Offin[g] for Boston. still fresher towards night in the same point—

15. Every thing rosy at Canso. Clappan[53] return'd with His Hay without interruption. no Indians Appear'd there.

Saturday 16th. the wind increas'd greatly, so much that the

Albany and fair Lady put back to Harbor—wind still in the same point—a Heavy Shower at two. Decreas'd at four—Warm.

Every thing else as Usual—talk of Indians certainly no danger. Right to be on Our Guard. No Indians Appear— Gone to the Eastward by Account.

Sunday 17th. An E[ast]rely Gale—somewhat cooler—but bright. Clear Weather.

Monday 18th. Sepr. A Council. threaten'd much by the Indians by Account—a Trader[54] at Chinicto attack'd by them. Kill'd seven Indians—three of the English Kill'd—this might have been a private pique but it looks not well. Every Account from Louisbourg confirms the Intention of the Indians against the settlement. the French at Lewisbourg pretend to clear themselves of sinister dealing but it is meerly to encourage Our Neutrals to stand out. They and Our Neutrals certainly support it. Hanfield[55] at Menis may probably be Attacked. Every thing as well as can be to receive them. What would we give now for a party of the St John's Indians—if they are not Dogs we need not fear the Mick macks &c. Clear.

2. Hopson How [?]—

Tuesday 19th Sepr. Went with Ives[56] on a Cruse. intend'd to go up the NW Branch[57]—met the Ulysess sloop. told us it was not safe as they had heard the Indians return'd. Yet wish I could have prevail'd to proceed As We have had such contradictory Accounts of this Branch. Capn Morris says it is not two mile one Half to the upper End of the Bason, and narrow opposite to Halifax not a Mile from our Citidal—an opening then to the Narrows absolutely proper if More. Met Gorham the Younger on His return from Canso St Peters &c—with His conference with the Indians—Mailiard presides over these, sent an Indian letter to the Governor to treat of peace and the Indians promise to come in person for that End—this looks well but I beleive not a word of it, a surprise is to be expected—somebody Knows for I find old Labrador was intrusted therefore suspect &c &c. Chebuctou head looks fine—why not Copper as In the Bay of Fundy? Rocky and Steep and a Vein is easyer found out in such Ground. Overturn'd in a Canoe with Rouse. Clear and Warm for the Season.

Ditto Pill &c &c—
An Account that the London is lost but gains no Credit.

Wenday 20th Sepr a Council on. Cook a fool but the stream too much against Him.[58] Clear and as usual till four. Rain with squalls at N W all even: A female fight &c &c.

Thursday 21st. clear but cold Morning and Even. Warm midday.
Friday 22^d. the Weather as before. Capn Howe Arrived—the Indians at Chignicto attempted an English trader. 7 Indians Kill'd and three English. the same Account with the former but confirmed by Howe.[59] The Indians of St Johns River confirm Our treaty with Howe. the Weather as before.

In continual expectations of the Indians. no sort of Intelligence of them since Gorhams letter from St. Peters wherein they promised to come with their grivances and proposals, but have not as I expected. this looks not well but surely we are strong Enough for Indians and the french dare not espouse them openly. this and no sort of intelligence makes me think that they will attempt to trouble us. better Intelligence certainly might be had with better Menagement.

Saturday 23^d. the weather as before. Din'd on shore with the Major.[60]

Letters propos'd to be sent to the french Governor at Lewisbourg since friday last on the Chignicto Affair &c—detained by contrary winds. Scot proposed—but fear

He will put aside for a f[rench]man. I think not. Scot more proper and especially so, as He is intend'd to reconn[o]itre Bay verte &c and other reasons.

Sunday 24th Sepr. Rather colder—a brisk Gale at N E.

Monday 25th. Cold with a misting rain. Din'd on the Hill. Showers all Day. set in hard for Rain at Night. Rains all night. the hardest Gale since we came.

Tuesday 26th—the rain continues with cold but the cold always less in proportion as the wind abates—the wind comes to the South. the rain continues.

Wensday 27th. Rain'd all last night Yet clear of Fogs. the Wind still High therefore cold. backs to the Eastward.

27th. did my Endeavour to make affairs easy with poor Cook.

Thursday 28. clear cold in the Morning. My Friend Scot sail'd without a scotch coajutor with the Ulyses and Casco, to Louisbourg Bay Verte &c—to return in three weeks if possible.

Friday 29th. Michaelmassday. The most clear and finest Day I have seen at the season—particularly Happy I could oblige a friend with ten Guineas &c &c.

I Know what to think of the Indians. They can not Essentially Hurt us—but their not appearing looks not well and those at St John's Isle under Mailiard not coming as they promised is worse. As Mailiard is suppos'd Our Friend—those under Lautrum [Le Loutre] are certainly determined against us, and without french and Scotch Knavery We may defy them all.

Saturday 30th. Major Guillman[61] Attack'd at His sawmill—six of His people clearing the River but two Hundr'd Yards from His fort shot at, one onely escap'd. the five butcher'd. He is supported. the Murther[er]s fled[62]—a great swell at South—yet all this affects not the settlers—they are in High spirits. Clear from fog and Warm.

Sunday the first of Octob^r. a Council Held. orders prepard to pursue the Indians and War declar'd.[63] God Allmighty prosper us—What for the St Johns Indians now? proposals of Wheat to retain them perhaps now too late—We have no intelligence of any Kind. Rangers necessary and Immediatly—Letters for Every body but me. surely nobody would detain my Letters and it is almost impossible that Every body should neglect me. Hetty must have wrote. why should not Tom? We cannot expect any Account now till spring. This with Everything almost breaks my Heart but this more than anything.

Monday 2^d Octr. the weather as yesterday. clear and warm at Midday. beating up for Voluntiers under Clappam. I wish them success for something immediatly should be done. the Governor went to His House on Shore. Major Guillman order'd to raise an Independant Company in Newengland[64] and to be with them Here in six weeks. Sail'd for Boston for that purpose. I am left in my old Hole on board the Beaufort. Davidson takes possession of the Cabbin. I care not. The Doctor[65] His lick spittle.

Tuesday 3^d Octb^r. Clear and Warm for the season. Din'd with Lawrance.

Book 2

[4 October 1749 to 15 March 1750]

Wensday Octr 4th. The Weather as Yesterday. Din'd with Foy[e]—nothing remarkable—

Thursday 5. Still fine weather. Cooks cause try'd before Howe.[1] White the Master of the Sphinx gone with an Armed Vessel to Mirlioneche[2] to Hunt for Indians and Cabbages—Labrador threatn'd. that falls hard on somebody. Guillman sails for Boston to raise a Company of Rangers. Howe and Cooloy return to Annapolis—A Grant given

Howe[3] by the Secretary—this surely is in my department of Bussiness—but let them do as they please.

Friday 6. nothing new. but rain at SE—the wind got to NW and the first frost I have seen tho not a Crown thick—the wind brings on the frost.

6. Lay at Cooks.

Saturday 7. the wind at NW. very Cold with frost. Dry over Head—on board—

Sunday Octr 8th. dry Over head but cold. the wind NW. In the Even: the Wind blew hard at SE. we drove[4] at five on Monday Morn. Oct[r] 9. near running on shore at Gorhams point.[5] at ten the wind came to the NW again—blows very hard and as we are not Moored may probably run ashore before Morn. not so cold as yesterday with frequent showers. No sort of news of either French or Indians.

Tuesday 10th Oct[r]. Cold. the Wind at NW. on board all day with Davidson the Doctor Clerks &c—

Wensday 11th. the weather Clears up. still NW. not colder than England. Din'd with the Governor. Came on board. a fine Night. Strange that we have no News but secrets are Kept from Me.

2 Wensday 11th.

Thursday 12 Oct[r]. clear and Dry with little frost.

Friday 13. the weather as before—

Saturday 14. A Council. the Ships to be continued all Winter and I think it quite proper, in case of any Accidents—as it will be long before we have ships from England—besides it will give us a better figure to the Enemy the french and Indians who might be prompted, if the shipping left us, to be troublesome. the Sphinx sailed at four this Afternoon for Madeira. Gates and I went in Her to Shamboro' Head[6]—return'd at ten and lay at the Governors on the Ground in Bulkeleys Room. the first time I lay on shore since I left Portsmouth. on the Ground &c. the weather clear and frosty—

Sunday Oct[r] 15th. the Weather as before.

Monday 16th—Rain and Cold. the Wind at SE. No News of Indians. Clear with frost—

Tuesday 17th Oct[r]. Clear with frost and cold. not colder than England—the Wind NW—a frost constantly at this time of Year Attends this wind—Rain and somewhat Warmer at SE. by a Letter from Capn Handfeild at Menis—the Indians pass'd by Pisigate[7] the 9th with the Prisoner taken at Guillman[8]—Not pursued by the party nor any other notice taken than to send the Account. All this foolish enough. suppose it true—and it is true.

> Nov[r]. Friday 24.
> No prisoner taken a[t] Guillmans. the poor fellow found a Month afterwards.

Tuesday 17th Oct[r]—to Tuesday 24th Oct[r]. the Wind shifting from SE to NW. at NW frosty and cold when the Wind is High, at SE, warm and pleasant when wind is not High. Cool if it blows with Rain and thick weather. Generally Clear at NW—

Thursday Oct[r] 19. Scot return'd from Lewisbourg with a Civil Letter from the Governor to Ours Avowing He did not Assist the Indians—Spoke to Mailiard who lik'd Scots proposal and wish'd for Leave to come Here—Saw no Indians at Canso. had a bad voyage and drove off His Station. the fishermen say the Most Stormy season they Ever Knew on this Coast.

Sunday Oct[r] 22[d]. the new Deputies sent from Menis—as we are at war with the Indians, we did not think proper to press the Oath to them—least they might refuse, and we have not force to Compell them. they drew a petition to the Governor of Lewisburgh that Mailiard might be Ordered their Priest Here—Whether Mailiard will be sent Here, or Whether He will be our friend if He does come I can not tell but force is requisite and nothing can be done Effectuall without it.

To Sunday Octr 29th. the Weather Variable as the Winds changed from NW to South East. not very cold but often strong Gales.

29 Octr. Times begin to Mend with Me and High time they should.

Monday Octr 30th. the Weather clear and fine. the Kings birth day—an Elegant ball at Court:[9]
To thursday Novr 2^d. the Weather still continues clear and fine so that the Inhabitants are hard at Work in making their Houses. This Day I left the Beaufort—and Lay in Gates's Closet. Mr Rumball and the boy at Mr Ewers House.

Thursday 2^d Novr. Cap^n Ewer sail'd in the Roehampton—with my Letters to Crane Tom Hetty and Wharton.

Friday the 3^d. the weather very fine and Clear.
Saturday 4th Novr. the wind at S. the weather still warmer and Clear. Ask'd Davidson for Money but None to be had. Strange all this.
Sunday 5th of Novr. the finest weather I ever saw any where on this Day.
Monday 6th. Continues warm but the wind coming to the S- heavy rains fell at night as usual.
Tuesday 7th. Clear and moderate—the wind came more to the N.

Tuesday 7th. recd a Letter from Hetty dated Sepr. 10th.

Wensday 8th. the wind at N. the first Hoar frost we have seen in this Country—Clear Sunshine at Midday. therefore warm. Shingling Mr Ewers House.
To Sunday Novr 19th—the Weather very moderate for the Season. the NW winds cold with a gentle frost. this Day a light Snow fell. therefore something warmer. Clear at Mid-

"A View of HALIFAX Drawn from y^e Topmasthead." Inset to "A Map of the South Part of Nova Scotia and it's Fishing Banks Engraved by, T. Jeffreys Geographer to His Royal Highness the Prince of Wales. 1750." Courtesy British Library.

day with sunshine. the frost likely to Continue. fell and Hurt my Hand coming from St Loes.[10] Mailiard talks of being Here in Spring with the Bishop of Canada's leave. the french order'd not to molest us or Encourage the Indians till further Orders from old France.

the Triumvirate[11] exposed. thank God. it is better with Me now.

To Thursday Novr 23. the frost continues. tho' supposed violent I can not think so. the weather by no means disagreeable—a fall of snow on tuesday.

Our treasury is shut up and no Money to be had till Scots return from new york. I wish He is not disappointed because I suspect methods are taken for that purpose. Delancy[12] at New York and Martin our plenipo' at Boston in league with the Sec-ry. the Secretary gives bills to Artificiers and Others. a fine paper Currency. All our Money carry'd to Boston because Mr Secretary will not give the price His plenipo' at Boston does. Here is profit to Martin and Company and rare monagomous for the Publick.

Scot sail'd for new york Octr 28.

Friday Novr 24. A thaw with rain. the Wind at SE tho' somewhat warmer yet not so pleasant as when it froze. Abundance of poor wretches starv'd in the snow by getting drunk and lying out. it can not be said that the severity of the weather could Kill any of them.[13] No news of Indians—and I think that bad—for Intelligence might be had if properly attend'd to—but nothing Will be done rightly till somebody is removed—what a Rascall this must be, my suspicions as Strong as Ever.

Saturday Novr 25—the wind at NW. froze hard again.

Sunday 26 Novr. Saturday night the coldest we have had this season. Major[14] says as cold as Ever He felt it at Lewisbourg—if worse it is tolerable.

Monday 27 Novr. frost continues.

Tuesday 28. Snows all Day gently as in England. the General Court Held.

Wensday 29th Nov[r]. frost again. the Court Continued and the Sessions End.

Thursday Nov[r] 30th. frost continues.

four and twenty Dollars taken [stolen?] out of the Stocking —the first Number 110.

Friday Dec[r] the 1st. a Gentle thaw without rain. at Home all Day. wrote to my Lord.

To Monday Dec[r] 11th. the thaw continues—with raw dirty Weather—but the 10th and 11th remarkably the finest Days I ever saw at the season of the Year.

Pill talk'd of as Coll:[15] not the first time so call'd—nor proud of the Honour.

Sunday the 10th. the Settlers order'd on the Parade to form a Militia.[16] at night a Courier from Minas—with an Account that Hamilton with twenty four Men taken without firing a Gun.[17] Strange this that a party should be thus surprised when by the account they were in a Marsh, so might have seen the Indians, got to their Arms and retreated—fir'd Seven Days at Handfields fort without doing the least Damage—No Account whether the fort returned the fire. Said to be about three Hundr'd joyned with the S[t] Johns River Indians and Chignictou—Rascalls that had made peace with Us—and Recd five Hundr'd pounds Ster. in presents. those certainly might have been secur'd at first as I have always Observed. Sat at the Committee to form some Laws and regulations of the General Court and Inferior—Drawing out a table of fees &c.[18] The Indians said to be retired with their Prisoners to Chignictou.

From Monday Decr 11th to Friday Dec[r] 15th—fine open weather—but the frost sets in Gently now.

Decr 11th. the Charlton sail'd, but put back to Cornwallis Isle[19]—and sail'd again the 14th[20]—My Letters to My Lord and Tom and Sir Lynch and poor Hetty—Under Majors Care[21]—an Attempt made to take the Profits of Colliers being register of Wills Attempted.

To thursday 21st. the frost continues with a two Inch snow on the Ground—very cold. the sky clear. had thirty pounds this Day from Davidson. Gorham return'd from Minas without action. the Indians went of[f] in twelve Canoes—no great force by that but this is supposed a party only. Wrote to Tom and Hetty by Majors Schooner. sail'd 20th. Order'd Wharton not to send the Goods to Rumball. Rumball leaves Me to go to Cook.

Friday 22^d Decr. frost with clear weather. put threescore Dollars into the stocking—

22^d. Rumball begs I would take Him again. Am fool Enough to Comply.

Saturday 23^d Decr. a thaw. the french come down with Cattle. some of them engage again In the works—

Sunday 24th—Very Warm for the Season. the thaw continues and the Ground clear of the Snow.

Monday 25th. Christmas Day. a small skim of frost. the weather mild and Clear. scarce a spek of snow on the Ground—As fine weather for the Season as Ever I saw.

Decr 26. Gorham gone in quest of the Indians by information. good luck attend Him. the first intelligence we have had.

To Friday 29th Decr.—the frost sets in severely again. the 28th. the coldest Day yet felt. Friday 29 a Gentle snow falls. much Warmer.

Decr. 29th. paid Rumballs bills. two pound five—took twelve Dollars today and twenty on the 26—Sixty at first.[22]

—To New Years day. small warm gentle falls of Snow this Day. as Mild with a thick fog as Ever I knew it for the Season—little or No Snow on the Ground. God bless the poor Hettys—and Grant that we may meet this Year. Provisions in plenty from Minas In lean black Cattle and poor Sheep.

To Saturday Jan^ry 6th. the frost sets In again very severely. colder I think than Ever. but no quantity of snow falls. Great talk that we shall be Attack'd by the Indians—which I fear is too true—our intelligence still very dark, tho' I am certain somebody Knows more of the matter than they will tell. Gorham took prisoners, three Pisequid French that had been in Arms[23]—whether right or No in Our circumstances I cannot tell—God send Us a Good deliverance from the Enemy and the severity of the Weather.

6 Jan^ry. took eight Dollars.

To Monday Jan^ry 15th—some days extreme cold when the wind is at NW with severe frost. Some days the Wind changes to SE. a thaw with pleasant Clear weather—but When Hazy a light snow falls—but by no means violent, as I had been taught to expect. the Militia form'd and Keep Guard in their several Quarters. barricading our selves in with engineers in every Quarter.[24] I Hope the best but the French quitting their work and going without their Money bodes not well for us. this day Jan^ry 15 clear and frosty with about six Inch snow on the Ground. Somebody Knows why the French Went.

Mem. Jan^ry 15. put twenty eight Dollars in a stocking in My book trunk. The Guard Kept in Mr Ewers house a great inconveniency to Me,[25] but it was done on purpose, and that I can not forget.

To Saturday Jan^ry 27th 1749-50. generally frosty—but with some mild thawing days—however the 22^d—23^d—the harbour froze up as High as Cape Sambro' there being no air to Keep the water in Motion—tho the frost was not near so severe as we have felt it this Year—the 25 a NW clear'd the Harbour—a gentle frost continues and today Saturday 27th it snows but gently. Wind at SW—Keep constant Guard—but no material intelligence of the Enemy and that is hard, and Keeps us in hot water—several schooners come in from Boston and Piscatoca [Piscataqua]—but no news from Guillman.

Saturday 27th. took four Dollars.

To thursday 1st of Febry 1749–50—frost with frequent gentle showers of snow as the Wind vary's from N to S—Snow not quite two foot Deep. We are in continual alarms about the Indians and french Attacking Us and without any sort of intelligence. It is hard that one poor french priest[26] should give Us this disturbance.

Thursday Febry 8. recd two Letters from Lord Halifax. Kind exceeding Kind—Three from the poor Dear Hetty's—God bless them and Grant that I may once More Embrace them. Lynch Elected without opposition for Denbighshire[27]—

To Friday 9th of Feb^{ry} 1749–50. very severe NW winds. consequently as cold as we have felt it this year but today Friday 9th—a clear warm day with a thaw—as pleasant as ever seen for the season—but I am far out of order to day, was bled—and Keep at Home at Mr Ewers. but this is very remarkable and came to my Knowledge this Day—that we have certain Intelligence that the Indians by the Assistance of the Canada French are fortifying near the Istmus of Chignicto.[28] this I always thought their threats of Attacking Us would end in—that we might not disturb them. All this we ought to have Known long since and should If proper encouragement had been given but thus it is. All the connivance in the world is given the Enemy and people are blind not to

see it, Nothing Known till the Enemy have done their
bussiness—Cobbs expedition too late—suppose care had not
been taken to blast it at Boston.[29] All those secrets hid from
Me—and still I Know them tho' not thro' the proper Channel. This is hard—but I shall be eternally Silent about their
Affairs.

To Wensday 14th—the wind returns to the NW as severe as
Ever—so that cold and a moderate Warmth depends on the
shift of the Winds—the S[t] Johns River Indians are supposed
to have quitted the Mickmacks—and a secret expedition on
which Bartello went today order'd. If it is possible the Enemy
will have notice. they never fail of proper Notice—Ours
always too late—What a Rascal![30]

> Valentines Day Dear Hetty—and I am all but Broken
> hearted—please God If I live I will never pass another
> without thee. I am now ill of a Jaundice—and am come
> Here to Ewers—that I may think of nothing but thee and
> My little Girl. God bless You both and grant that we may
> once More Embrace again. Surely the last proposal I sent
> you and Tom will take place. Send it My Lord. I depend
> Wholely upon it.[31] thou must never come Here and I can
> not Stay without thee—Was Every thing Here such as I
> could wish it—but no such thing. My Employ is curtail'd
> dayly—by M[r] Secretary who is All in All—I bear it very
> hardly and it Hurts my Health. My Head Aches or I would
> write to thee to day. God bless You both. Amen.

To tuesday Feb[ry] 20th—the weather continues severe as cold
as any this season with a great fall of snow—so that we have
it now full three foot Deep—but today the weather takes a
more favourable turn—the Wind at S and Yet Clear—

To thursday 22[d] Feb[ry]—the finest weather I ever saw for the
season, with the strongest sun. the night quite Clear with a
sharp frost—and today Wensday 22[d] seems as if a thaw
would come On. No longer fears of an Invasion from Indians
or French. today twenty Horse load of Hay came in from
Menis—I Know no secrets but that Bartello is on His march

to cobequid—and Cobb proceeds on His expedition to Bay Verte—but all this secrecy from Me is stuff. I Know somebody Else can Inform the Enemy better. therefore am of opinion that both expeditions will be fruitless. God forgive Me if I think unjustly of any Man.

To Saturday 24th Feb^{ry} 1749-50. the brightest finest weather Ever seen. a strong sun in the day—a little cake of frost at Night—

Sunday 25 Febry. A thaw set in with rain at night and a Hard Gale at night at SW.

Monday 26. the thaw continues which took off one third of the snow, the snow being three foot Deep—and this caus'd a land flood which would have Hurt our Houses but a small catch of frost came on Tuesday 27 Feb^{ry}—and continues with clear weather till saturday March 3^d 1749-50.

March 3^d. very hazy. wind at SE, a light snow with a thaw. No News from Bartello. I wish all is well with Him. The french come dayly to M^r S[ecreta]ry and Our Governor not acquainted with it. All this strange particularly May [March] the 2^d He met two of them Himself. Engrosses all the Trade[32]—Complaints made of that. &c &c—

Saturday March 3^d. 8 at night Bartello arriv'd with Girard the Priest at Cobequid and the Deputies but Charlvroy[33] went off twelve Hours before as another of the name told Bartello—so that they had intelligence as I suspected.[34]

to tuesday March 6th. light frosts at night. the sun thaws in the Day—sometimes light snows but by all appearance the winter is breaking Up. yet still cold with the wind at NW.

To Thursday March 15—light frost at night. strong sunshine in the Day. the snow wearing away.

Book 3

[17 March to 5 April 1750]

March 17th. heavy Rains in the Morn. Wind at South, fogy

All Day. a strong thaw. the only rain we have had since Sunday 25 Feb[ry].

To March 25th Lady day 1750.[1] Foggs with light rain, some times clear sunshine with a Mild air—the frost and snow decreasing Hourly—scarce any in the town, tho' not yet gone out of the woods. the Annapolis and Minas people Call this a long winter with more snow than Common. Thank God it is now over.

Monday 19th March. Rogers[2] sail'd where I can not tell. some Indian secret expedition, to Chignicto perhaps to give Cobb the meeting. Rouse has the Dove sloop.[3] not sailed Yet. I heartily wish Every expedition success, but doubt 'em greatly. for secret as our expeditions are to Me—I fear the Enemy Know to[o] much Our Intentions.

to Wensday 28th March. the Weather variable from foggs and light rain, to Mild sunshine. this Day wensday 28th Heavy rain. Cobb Arriv'd Here March 26th with near seventy Men. His expedition stopt by Order at Boston the moment He intend'd to sail. this day the fair Lady sail'd for England. Gorham wound'd at the attack at Pisequid. no one Kill'd. The Enemy drawn of[f]. Clappams Rangers and St Loes Company of Philips's March to His assistance. Bourns[4] schooner came in March 26th with the first fare of Fish.

My Gun and Box came with Cobb. Wrote to My Lord Crane Tom and Hetty by the fair Lady.

March 30th 1750. the Governor in council resolv'd on an expedition to Chignictou.[5] to March to Minas to take Gorhams Clappams and Guilmans rangers—with St Loes and fifty of Warburtons[6]—and there embark on board Rouse and several light Armed Sloops—for Chignictou. in all four Hundred Men—the Command given to Major Lawrance. My Friendship with the Major and Love for the Cause determined Me to Attend the expedition which Major Lawrance is much pleased with, and the Governor by no Means dislikes. I shall now see whether the French have had intelligence of this and satisfy all suspicions. but whether they have had intelligence or No—please God we are Strong Enough to bring them to reason. And Grant O God that in the whole of this transaction I may behave so as to give me self satisfaction, that I may be the more worthy to embrace thee, My Dear Life. God bless thee and the poor little Girl, and Grant that we may once More meet, never More to part—Amen.

Tuesday April 3d. Rouse sailed with the sloops—fine Weather—

Wensday 4th April. I Close up my Journal till my return. please God I may Have My Health. We March at ten on tomorrow being April 5th 1750—Grant me thy Grace O God and success—Bless O God My Wife and Child. I fear not, having an Humble Hope in a Happy Eternity—thro' thy Infinite Goodness and Mercy O God and the Mediation of Christ Jesus—My Saviour.

fifteen Guineas in My Purse.

Book 4

[5 April to 13 May 1750]

Thursday April 5th 1750.[1] the Detachment for Chignictou went in boats to Sackville Fort. no Room there. march'd half a Mile into the Woods and encamped[2]—

Friday 6th. March'd and encamp'd in the Woods that night. nothing extraordinary but a dull alternative of beech and other white wood on the Ground. least moist in the swamps. the fir of all Kinds very thick but the timber not large—several lakes but Know nothing How large they Are—no great assents [ascents] nor any Rivers of note—except a few black water brookes from one lake to another.

Saturday 7th—arriv'd that night at the five Houses on the River St Croix. before we got there—at about five miles distance came down a very long desent to the River Ardois—from this Hill to the River Ardois, the Country much alter'd. small beech and birch on the Hill—a shaly soil. most certainly Mineral[3]—and near the River an attempt seems to have been made in the mining. the vale deep and Narrow and the assent perpendicular almost in some places—with a Greyish look on the broken land, where the Minerals might be discover'd—in the vale the largest Pines I ever saw—and the land as good as any possibly can be, the stream clear with a fine Gravel Bottom—in going near two Mile we assend into excellent gravel land clear and with a good Coat. Half a Mile further on the Descent are the first Houses of the Pisequid division, we descend then into good Meadow land—where the St Croix River falls in—* we cross'd that River over a new bridge made by Gorham after His late action Here. on a fine rising Ground Good Land above the meadows the Houses Are—Even this land looks mineral tho' the surface is so Good.

*Here are Saw Mills and a Corn Mill.

Sunday 8th. Arrived at Cap^n St Loes camp on the Pisequid River, Call'd Baban.[4] now every little village in each particular District is call'd after the name of the Clan and these are many. we march'd th[r]o' a shrubby wood Country for three Hours—and this Country also seems mineral—then we open'd a fine Champion[5]—with skattering Houses—that resembled greatly Northamptonshire but the land Much better and this continu'd to the very banks of the River of Pisequid. this River carry's a great deal of Water and the Tide rises near sixty foot. at Low water we waded thro' this River for the Channel is wide—not quite so wide as that at Conway[6]—Marsh lands Here for about a Mile—then the Champion rises gradually, and about half a Mile further we found St Loe encamped near a neat french Chappel.[7] Excellent Land.

Monday 9th April. arriv'd at the Stone House on the Grand Prie Minas. in this March the Champion continu'd two Hours. then we fell into a shrubby bottom with clear rivilet.

from thence we assend'd for two Hours and More—More than three Hours. very high land. the wood small tho' frequently met immense large trees lying rotting—or standing dead and without bark—this High land is fork'd and a clear river runs thro' the Middle. from Hence we descend'd gradually till we came to the River Gaspero—the tide equally Here as at Pisequid—the River very narrow so we were obliged to pass in Canoes and bad one—but we had no misfortune thank God—from Hence two miles to Grand Prie consquently an up and down Hill tho' Gradual. Grand Prie Minas stand like Ruddlan[8] with a Much larger Marsh but this diked in and plow'd. As they call the District Minas I fancy the Mines must have been on the bank of the Gaspero as that is High and steep, and I though[t] I perceiv'd on on[e] of them the looks of an old work not but that the rising Ground above the[re] looks Mineral.[9] We never went out of our ranks least the Enemy might have taken advantadge and truely in Millions of places twenty Men might have anoy'd us greatly—

Tuesday 10th. dined at handfeilds Fort at the Entrance of the Gasporo into the Bason of Minas—I cannot number the Rivers that fall into this Bason. My Chart will show them. Lay in a barn last night and have not had my Cloaths off. Thank God I am in Good Health and Grant us success.

Wednesday 11th. loundging at Minas in expectation of Rouse. it is unlucky He does not come for our expedition takes air,[10] and doubtless the Enemy will have advice of Us and be prepared. delightfull spring weather but the inhabitants seem to neglect their Husbandry. the Marsh is near three leagues over from Grand Prie when very High land bounds the Eye that runs out into a bluff in the Bason.

the Marsh to the Wood is only about two mile a Cross—this wood low land—Marsh lands again to the River Les Habitant that runs under the High lands that continue to Annapolis—but in the Bason of Minas ends in a bluff point[11] like Penryndâ.[12] but Higher land Mineral without Doubt. there is another bluff point in the Bason on the Cobequid side that native copper is found on and some little silver as I am inform'd—the River Canard runs paralell with the Les Habitant.

Pisequid is much a more pleasant Country I think and hath equally the advantadge of a navigable River and being without that large Range of Marsh besides the Bason must be much warmer in winter. the inhabitants here live very sparingly, at least so now we are Here as not caring to discover their stores—we had a few small smelts and a fish they call the Gasporo not unlike a Herring in look but differing in taste and rose on my stomack for twenty four Hours—

This day a party went out to secure arms to refit Gorham's that lost His in the Action, and tho' we promise to pay for them, or return them, or give them others—Yet the inhabitants are affected with it. Every proceeding is extremely critical for the Inhabitants are on the balance now either to go or stay, and that is of great consequence to us, for if they go they will greatly reinforce the French, which is the great design of DLutre [Le Loutre]. If they stay, tho' they are not hearty in our interest, they are not actually against us—which they must be if they quit the Province and truely they are a great body of people. Now the question is—whether for thirty arms or such a trifle (for they are not wholely disarmed) It is most Eligble[13] to venture the disgust of the Inhabitants. In my opinion, in our situation, I would not.

Thursday 12. No Rouse yet, but two small trading vessels with Rum &c one of them Gordon from Boston Martins brother in Law[14] and merchant Magee—I know who both these are in partnership with and it is no wonder Philips's Corps is in disgrace[15] as by the Winnits[16] they interfere in this trade. one of these Winnits is now Here in a sloop with Goods &c—

Friday 13—Saturday 14. Phillips arrived in His schooner.[17] no news of Rouse. the Deputies with their Priest assembl'd at the Head Quarters to desire leave to go to the Governor for their dismission out of the Province. The Inhabitants have left their Houses and there is a suspicion of the Enemy being at Hand. We are here naked and exposed to All the fire they can make, and I doubt not but that if an Attack was made by the Indians the French would Join.*

*then greatly our superiors in Number.

In this condition would it not be proper to draw nearer Handfields Fort, or go into the Fort—for then we might chuse our Time of acting whereas we must be under apprehensions of being Attack'd at the Enemy's Option, particular in the night time which is their constant method of acting. besides our destination is not Here. we ought to Keep our forces entire for Chignictou, and as soon as Rouse arrives we must go to the fort to embark.

In an Enemys Country the Forces of the same Prince should always unite—and take Every advantadge that may offer for their safety, I mean so far as to have it in their power of Offer Battle when convenient: and be able to decline it, if not, in security.

To close the whole, should the Enemy make a Head[18] we are not Here to attack them but had we the shipping to make what Haste we could to Chignictou and fortify there—when their forces lay Here. Nothing can be said against this reasoning but a false notion of valor, which a commander Ought to Despise—His bussiness is to procure for Himself and Troops all the safety the Nature of the service will permit. Holding the enemy too cheap is the Rant of a Volunteer.

Is it possible that the disaffection of the Minas inhabitants was unknown to the person that conversed so constantly and secretly with them? If Known why not discovered? that we should come here and find things thus—and told the contrary at Halifax is strange. Every turn convinces Me the fellow is a Rogue &c.[19]

Sunday April 15th. Easter Sunday. God Grant Us Success. Rouse Arrived with the Dove and Philips schooners.[20] talk of delaying the embarkation on account of the disaffection of the Inhabitants till further Order. Yet determin'd afterwards to proceed—and that certainly right corresponding with the Instructions &c.

Monday 16th. went to Gorham at the Fort and observe a bill of His return'd by Davidson. two of trade &c. Excellent directions drawn up by Gorham. proposals thought to be sent to the Gov'. to excuse the inhabitants from taking arms &c as a Method to Keep them in the province. if sent the result will be too late for us, particularly in the immediate Action, As the King of France interests Himself so much in the affair—as the Priest says—and no wonder as it will be of infinite service in His Colony's and Hurt us Much, for one of the present Inhabitants are worth a Dozen Europeans—took up Winnits schooner on the service at which He boggled much—said to be in the french Interest by Rouse and Gorham. Spleen perhaps, still two of a trade &c. propose to embark on Wensday. I wish we may. that is Our destination. I love the Major and hope All success and Honor may attend the expedition. An action I think we must certainly expect at Landing and Every night we are Here I expect a surprise, therefore the sooner the better we are at our destination and the enemy are certainly fools not to interrup[t] us Here: naked as we are, not to be assisted by the fort or shipping.

Tuesday 17th. nothing extraordinary.

Wensday 18th. March at Eleven to the fort in order to embark—God Grant us success. at 4 afternoon embark'd in 6 Transports with the Albany[21]—at 7 under way. Cape Fendu[22] and Cape porcupine make a little Bason that takes in the Rivers Cobequid, St Croix, Gasporo, Le Habitant and Canard.

at a Head Land between Minas and Cobequid called Cape Fiandi. Copper Oar most certainly. Davidson sent no Rum for the troops on the Government Contract, but sent Gordon with a Cargo to supply us in this our Absolute necessity at the rate He could get. We know ye partn[er]ship. better take it from miller[23] if equaly cheap with Gordon

Also for Money refer'd to Magee[24] another in partnership. this is strange but He must take us for fools. St Loe refer'd for Money to pay his Company either to Magee or Gordon, to draw for the Dollars payable either at Halifax or Boston. this Gordon vessel is armed out of the Gov^t. stores—the Guns Cap^n Rogers will swear to and the small arms belonged to the Company Cobb raised at Boston. upon what account He has those Arms I can not tell. Cobb bought them for the expedition, brought the Men, but left those arms—and now we are in want of arms. If they pretend to have bought 'em they must have bought them at Half price, but why should we sell them when in want of Arms our selves—but beleive they were not bought but taken at pleasure by Martin—this is Horrid Doing, and yet those poor fellows the Capns dare not say a Word.

Thursday 19th. at Anchor of[f] cape Porcupique—Pork Epicque—why at anchor? forc'd to send to Gordon for Rum for the people[25] and right between the Pisequid River and Petit Riviers is the Cape Feundu call'd by the inhabitants where there is Copper—and a little Island near shore call'd paint Island[26]—certainly mineral—but the land from the Pisequid River to Cobequid is but Low in comparison of Cape pork Epicque. High land from thence to Anapolis. a fog till about ten. clear after. the air sharp. the water Muddy with ye violence of the tides—came thro the Gut in the night and anchor'd about twelve near Spencer Island—Squaly with Foggs. Spencers Island a round High small Island with shrubs very near the shore—therefore Woody as every where Else. the bluff near Spencers Island Higher than Cape Doree and this bluff make[s] a little Bay like Nevin[27] and Portmillson[28]—on this Cape Dorée and to the other Bluff is native Copper. This we sail'd by on Friday April 20th. at Eleven o clock forenoon of[f] Cape Chignicto. this with Doree makes another Bay Deeper than the other two—I observe no Rivers to fall in Here but little Gullies—the shore land is steep and Broken and in those cliffs the Native Copper is found in Plenty—the Broken land is of different Colours—and I am told consist of a soft crumbling stone—some of a bleuish Cast like Mar[b]le some a Dirty red—we are between Holt Island [Ile Haute] and the Main. Holt Island is partly round and High about three leagues in the Channel, is steep and Broken as the Main. Shrubbs on both. no large sands Here nor Rocks. the navigation not worse than Bristol Chanel, and perhaps the tide equal to what we have Here.

Letters came by Philips Dated 16th Monday but none to the Major or says so. I know what to make of this—some grand secret and I expected no secrets Now.

at 4 oclock afternoon off apple River. the passage the St John Indians take to Cobequid to cross Chignictou Channel. six leagues the scale will show—the land from Cape Chignicto not so High as before—the opposite shore rather Higher.

Smoke on Cape Rouge. the land low with a fine bite in shore—the land rises behind it up in Country and remarkable High Land above Shepordy [Shepody]— off Shepordy near two Leagues Grin[d]stone Island—larger than Isle Holt. the High Land call'd Shepordy Mountain. Deep Vallies appear in the Mountain. at five the village of Shepordy in sight. Grinstone Isle of [f] the Bason of Shepordy. the land still low on Cape Chignictou side and on the other side the Gut. at six afternoon entring the Gut of Chignictou. within this Gut on Cape Chignictou side—Shaly Rocks on the sea shore with very strong veins of Coal.[29] at about eight afternoon come to an Anchor under the Shelter of small point, rather on the Chignictou side of the Gut. a fine Clear Day. the night promising. Heard firing as at the village of Chignictou. no particular Haste now requisite as we can Hope for no particular success by surprise as the Enemy have sufficient intelligence—for we observe the smoke signals all the way we come up. A proposal made, and intend'd to be executed, to send thirty men on shore this night in the Whale boats—to take some of the Inhabitants of a village at some distance from Chignicto to tell us the posture they are in. Gorham Clappan [Clapham] and Cobb attempted it but forc'd to put back the wind being too High.

Rain from twelve friday night till nine Saturday Morning 21st April and the wind still continues High: at Eleven fore-noon, the rain gone of[f] but not likely to Hold, Weather Continu'd so bad not possible to Land had we known the posture of the Enemy and that certainly necessary before such a thing could be attempted—at 2 afternoon saw a fire in the town—sent Cobb with a proper Letter to the Deputies with Landri the Minas Man.[30] the flames increas'd at their approach and continues till now past eight. the wind so High not possible to Land our people this night to take an inhabitant for information. Those people certainly now determin'd against Us and desperate. the policy therefore to let them go and Bay Verte is open to them.

Sunday 22d. went from the Albany on board Cobb to Land at six in the Morn: Land'd Our Men at eight on a Meadow on the left seaward of Chignicto without either Accident or Op-position. When the Men were forming a White flag on a Dike appear'd*—

*at about a Quarter of Miles distance still on the left of us on our Approach

which was suppos'd to be a flag of truce or parley—Scott went up, and said two peasants set it up as the boundary of the French Kings Dominions—but that an officer was coming from La Corn[e]. when the officer appear'd the Major sent Him a Message by Scott that it was the Governors Order La Corne should quit the province or be treated as an Incen-diary—the officer reply'd as from La Corne not to do any thing rashly and that La Corne would come Himself, with in-tent to treat & Lay His Comanding officers Orders before Him. at the first of our approach the Mass House and several others were in flames. During this parley I propos'd to the

Major my returning* with Cap^n Rous to the Albany and told
Him my reasons—Now I never repented any thing more in
my Life—Least the Major should give it a bad construction. I
value not what swaggering volunteers will say, for I take no
pride in verbal Courage—but the want of proper Courage
was not my Motive. what I propos'd to do perhaps I may fail
in and please God will be with the Major in the Morning. when I left the Camp at Eleven forenoon there seem'd
no Appearance of an Action, as La Corne had promised to
come to an explanation with the Major.

*If the Major had conceiv'd my going off with Capt Rous
in a unfavourable Light, or Suppos'd any body Else would
have taken it [in] that Light, it was unkind In Him not to
tell me. I press'd the point. I went on as far As Able, and
press'd another which would have been of signal service,
the sending Rouse's long boat Man'd in the Night to bring
of[f] an Inhabitant to Know the situation and Strenght of
the Enemy.

the Day Chill and windy with heavy showers. La Corne
seems to have a picketed fort in that part He calls the French
Dominions*.

*We found the Enemy ready to receive us in all form. La
Corne in His picketed fort so large as must have been the
work of time—the disaffection of the Minas inhabitants
must have been Known at Halifax and thro' them the
preparations made Here to support the pretend'd right of
the Grand Monarque—and by this disaffection of the Inhabitants we must have fought a Whole Country greatly
populous and Us'd to Arms and in point of amunition well
supply'd. In a country the most difficult to Attack the
Enemy and that without the least Knowledge of the Country—with the apparent risque of starving—as it was possible for the Enemy to Cut of[f] our Communication with
the Transports, had we endeavour'd the least advances
upon them. it is very hard it should always be thus—that
the Actions of the Enemy shew plainly their Knowledge of
our very Intentions. besides according to Bartelo L'Corne

had made His dispositions in a soldierlike Manner
—Mann'd well the Dyke on which He fix'd His Flag, that
was equal to any entrenchment. with Indians had His own
Corps in reserve on the wind mill Hill with a wood on His
Left and a River on His Right, at about the Distance of a
Quarter of a Mile from His Picketed Ground before mention'd—the Assylum for All the Rebel inhabitants. Now
we had nothing but Small Arms nor a possibility of getting
our Cannon or Shells to dislodge them. We might have
fought but could never have made a proper Impression—In His circumstances and Ours.

4 afternoon the town still burning. Grant Our Major and
poor Men Success O God. the Inhabitants are certainly ir-
reconcilable to burn All—and in this fury Hope they will not
join the Enemy—My proposing the Errand to return with
Rouse and failing in the Success may be constru'd to my
discredit—but it arose from the fear I was in about the Sloops
and the Countenance He might give them and the Whole expedition—never thinking of the Invidious turn that may be
given it, besides the dread I am In about the Success of Our
troops—that Hours never pass'd in greater uneasyness than
Now. please God I will be with them in the Morn.

at twelve at Night the Major return'd with all the troops
reimbarked, as not possible to proceed further or entrench
there, La Corne with His Indians and troops at Hand to suc-
cour the Inhabitants—whose inhabitants in this Fury determined to Join Him.

Monday 23^d. Resolv'd Unanimously to return to Minas, (as a
piece of service most usefull for Common Cause, In those our
present circumstances) to stop the Inhabitants there and at
Pisequid from Joining the Enemy and carrying of[f] their Effects.[31]

If a Rebel inhabitant could be taken, without much risque,
or impediment to Our resolution 23^d I think would be of
service that we might learn fully their strength and determination.

Monday 23[d]. in our return came near the Coast on the St Johns River side almost opposite to Apple River, very Craggy, for now I was near enough to see it in High Lands. Morrass between with rocky Clumps. the points to the sea broken and Craggy tho not High. it is in the inland the Ground rises. in the breaks of the Land rivilets running down cover'd with wood as usual.

Still rocky High Lands with shrubs with deep Cliffs and strong rivilets like tany balch.[32] anchor'd at seven after noon within a League of Apple River—Night promising fine. all Day frequent showers—with light fogs. rather Cold.

at ten on tuesday April 24th not able to turn Cape Chignicto. at Anchor near Isle Holt to Stem the tide. a very fine Day, the only tolerable weather we have had since we left Minas. at four afternoon a fresh breeze. favourable. weigh anchor. Cape Chignicto and Cape D'orr make a Small Bay. Anchord Under Spencers Island. a very stormy night with violent rowling—

Wensday 25th. rainy dark weather. weigh'd anchor at eight forenoon. blows gently. Clumpy uneven stony land on the Main near Spencers Isle—all this Country seems Mineral. Anchor'd under Cape Pork a picque—could make no way this day—Wind and tide against us.

Thursday 26th—at Anchor under the Cape at 8 oclock in the Morning. at five afternoon return'd to our old Quarters Grand Prie. recd our Letters at Handfields fort. Dispatch'd Answers to 'em.

Friday 27th—loundging at Grand Prie as before—the weather dry, but Cold for the season.

Saturday 28. at three in the afternoon on board the Dutchess with Coll. Gorham for Annapolis[33]—made no way that night but went on board the Albany and hasten'd Joseph Gorham and Cobb on their expedition to pick up an Inhabitant at Cobequid. at Eleven forenoon on sunday April 29 at Anchor under Cape porkypique. the weather

Squaly and Cold for the season. on the opposite shore between porkypique and Fendu a fine Cove—and a little more towards Spensers a Ledge of Rocks. this opposite shore Under Patent to Duke Chandois.[34] anchor'd near Spensers Isle at Six Morn:

April 30th Monday. under sail with a fine breeze and good tide. breeze continues till noon, and we make some little way Even against tide. Spring weather with rain.

From May 1st to the 7th Monday at annapolis. entertaind at the several families—a Compleat Garrisson. Mascarene very obliging. Wrote to My Lord by way of Boston, Sealed packet with Rogers for Boston.

"A Prospect of Annapolis Royal in Nova Scotia, 1751." Water-colour by Thomas Chamberlain after J.H. Bastide. Courtesy Public Archives of Canada.

May the 7. The Cape a sandy high land between two Rivers—the largest runs a great way into the Country and is well inhabited. the Country not much cleared Even Here, so long inhabited. the people content themselves with Dyking out the Marsh. Several of the Dykes down about Annapolis—Gardens on the Cape—pretend to Gardening but no conjures.[35] on the other River Saw Mills and a salmon fishery—a foolish way of catching fish by diging Holes in the gravel a little above High water Mark—No Notion of Wares [weirs]. the Annapolis French I yet think will not go. Expect terms &c. Howe their friend. Money to be got out of us. Winnit gone to St Johns to trade opposite to the Mouth of the Gut and bear River opposite to the Gut landwards. the Priests agree they live Happier than could be imagin'd—plenty of Every thing with Respect &c. At ten at Night I went on board the Squril for Halifax.

May 8 tuesday. at 9 forenoon turning thro' the Gut. High land on both sides—no large timber onely exactly in the Gut. the land a little High. the opening to the Gut low but rocky. it is wrong that Winnit is gone to trade at St Johns for the Indians are always poor in spring and might have brought them to a peace perhaps. Howe is concern'd in this for money &c. either by peace or supplying the Indians—the indians this war said not to be so cruel as formerly. open Petit Passage at 4 afternoon. broken lands with Island till we make Cape St Mary's. call one Salusbury Isle.[36] Bay St Marys is as large as anapolis and runs near it a small Cleriage place between 'em. the land therefore that makes this side of the Bay Narrow. light winds with rain. Petit Pasage Narrower than Annapolis Gut. Deep water.

Tuesday 8 May. small winds all Day. Calm at night with rain.

Wensday 9 of May. at 9 in the Morning by long Island. the passage between long Island and Salusbury Island makes the Grand Passage as between Salusbury Island and the Main petit passage. Calm and Clear. about noon the wind Sprang up Contrary So that we could not get round long Island but forc'd to put back into grand passage and come anchor at Cove on long Island—there is small island in the middle of the passage which makes very Narrow. walk'd cross a Morass on long Island but saw no game. the wind abates somewhat.

Thursday May 10th. at Anchor in the passage. Wind Still contrary. Hazy weather. at twelve out the way we came In. the wind would not permit us to go thro' which would have sav'd 5 leagues thro' St Marys Bay. Strange there is nothing of[f] this Shore. Met a High Sea. lay too to fish. caught Cod of[f] Salusbury Isle. Out at Sea all night. rather Stormy.

Friday 11 May. Stretching for Cape Sable. could not put in to Ponbonco [Pubnico]. the Wind Contrary. at one the tusket Islands three in Number—We pass between these tuskets an[d] Seal Island. a favourable breeze with half Ebb. in this pass the Strongest tide Ever seen insomuch we had a great Sea and each tide smo[o]th water. at sea all night in almost a Calm.

Saturday May 12th. a small breeze at ten in the Morning. Still between four and five leagues from Cape Sable. expect the tide of Ebb to bring us round—saw several small craft in their way to Boston. the Breeze freshen'd greatly and we ran all night. at 9 at night very near running foul a brig: and we must have perish'd.

on Sunday May 13 of[f] L'Have the very land we first made in the Sphinx.[37] it is an Island at L Have that makes the Harbor and the time we Anchored we were certainly in St Margarets.[38] the Green Island Lying there with a Ledge between that and the Island that had Shrubs upon it—of[f] L Have 9 in the Morning. Three in the afternoon a brest of Cape Sambro' with a gentle breeze Thank God. a small Cove exactly at the turn of the Cape. half a League to Westward a small rocky Island. looks clear as if sandy. a passage between that and the Main—the Island a White Rock. looks sandy as does the Shore. a good berth necessary in turning the Cape without a Good Pilot.[39]

Book 5

[13 May 1750 to 19 April 1751]

Sunday May 13th. Thank God arriv'd at Halifax at five after-noon after the Chignicto expedition. recd a Letter from poor Hetty and Crane at Annapolis. We had no fogs in sailing from Anapolis Here. During the expedition some rain with intermediate Warm Days—May Continues very rainy. Yet fine spring weather for this Country for except the rains fall this Month there must be a scarcity of Grass.

May 25th. Davidson went for Boston.[1]

June the 1st. very Warm. continues So with refressing Showers at intervals that if we had Grassland Every thing must grow. till June the 8th Friday.

> June 1st. Maugers Sloop Arriv'd with a box of Cloath much too fine[2] and Letters from the poor Hettys with a Letter of Credit from Tom on Mauger.
>
> Mem: at a Council held May 20th. press'd by Davidson to take the power out of the peoples Hands to chuse Depu-ties. why press that if we propose their Stay? to irritate the people too far may better answer the ends of the French. I am not at All surprised at L[ord] Halifax's account of our Secretary. the Priests live very well among the people. Tell that to Crane. also to rejoyce at L[ord] Halifaxs conquest, the conspicuous Light it puts Him in &c. prevail'd to Carry the Cut to the N West river into Execution &c. but does not go On so briskly and perfectly as it might. the Indians coming on may quicken it.[3] An out Guard there would be of the utmost security to the Town. No ships as Yet arriv'd or we might have done good Service.

To June 20th. fine weather with showers at proper season. very Hot to day. last year by all accounts this spring season was very dry. Tomorrow is the Aniversary of our arrival in this port. thank God I am in health and bless my poor wife and Child and Grant we may once more meet again. David-son not return'd from Boston &c[4]—Certain Accounts that the

Indians are about. lost five Men at the Narrows.[5] the Major goes on well at Pisiquid. He supposes the French in better Humour. No foggs except one Day as Yet come into the Harbor. the fishing goes on very well.

Chignictou possessed &c. the French have this opportunity to strengthen themselves and poyson the Inhabitants. the great Mans negotiations at the Court of Boston must be weighty—His Magnificence &c. suppose He clears the Clod[6]—not impossible. if not His several branches of Trade will be settled to His Advantage. His Sub[7] propos'd the register Clerk to M[r] Secretary. if so M[r] Register must clear the Clod. I Know this has been long a brewing. not unlikely as things are so partially carry'd in His favour. tell this to Crane. Major Lawrence extream friendly. does very well at pisequid. I am let into no State Secrets, and bussiness seemingly industriously Kept from Me. the Coxcomb Still Keeping His Court at Boston. the Scotch Pedlar and Gays Monkey[8] mistaken for the Man of Bussines and fine Gentleman. Rous and Bulkeley a Match perhaps.

Sunday June 24th. the fine weather continues. rather Hot. no fogs. this day, at fort sackville with Cotterel. Rogers arriv'd from Boston in the Ulyses—two Sloops of War for Our Service Arriv'd There Orderd by Rous,[9] one of them into the Bay of Fundy—and High time. Rogers met a french Vessell full of men from Louisbourg sailing into the Bay. the other order'd Here to be sent for Bay Verte. Rouse comes with Her with M[r] Secretary perhaps.

Monday and tuesday 25th 26th June. rain 25 Morn. the Wind comes Eastward of the N. and blows very Hard. 26th. the Roehampton anchors below Cornwallis Isle furthest beech. Ewer arrives. thank God poor Hetty is well. recd a Letter from Her and Crane. My Lord and He at Bath. Cold but fine fish weather. No fogs with this Storm.

Wensday 27th. clear fine weather returns.

To July thursday 5th. this day A very strong Sun but the breeze makes it tolerable. the Anniversary of the first tree cut

Here. No fogs come As Yet into the Harbor except on tuesday and wensday last but not so to Hurt curing Our fish. the fishery goes on surprisingly. eight thousand Quintal of fish Now ready for Market. Mʳ Davidson return'd from Boston tuesday July 3ᵈ—Lord Colvill[10] in the Success arriv'd that Day.

to July 21ˢᵗ. Hot scortching weather. not a drop of rain nor fog in the Harbor. banks of fog without—within this time order'd by the Governor one of the Inspectors of Mʳ Davidson's Accounts[11]—what I much disliked ((viz) Whether He traded on the Publick Credit or His Own) as improper for Me, Never having been let into the secret of Publick affairs—on the Contrary an affected Secrecy in those Affairs always Held towards me. Wrote by the Sarah to My Lord, Crane, Sʳ Lynch, Tom and Hetty.

Sunday July 22ᵈ. My Friend Major Lawrence Arrived from Pisiquid. Lieut Hussey[12] has the Care of My Letters. the Scott Suspect. I hope they will not detain them. Yet every thing is to be suspected from that Quarter.

Monday July 23ᵈ. the Montagu[13] launched.

to Wensday 24ᵗʰ. Wind NE—rain very acceptable but it fell not so Heavy as last Year, and Strong fogs Home into the Harbor—but luckyly few fish can Suffer as the last fairs [fares] are much harden'd and fresh ones not come In. the wind being Contrary the Sarah Still at the Mouth of the Harbor.

To August Thursday 1ˢᵗ 1750. the Weather less Hot than before the rain fell, and very pleasant. light fogs when the wind goes to SEly but not so thick as last Year, and small showers of rain, yet we should want More had we tillage. this day arriv'd that part of the Govʳˢ regiment[14] expected from newfoundland and a large schooner with 160 adventurers from Ireland. the Montagu sails today to ballast at the Saw Mill.

To August Monday the 13th [12th]. Seasonable proper weather with refreshing moderate showers. The rains I think fall not so heavyly as last year. Lasselle's regiment[15] from ireland arrived within this time in six transports all in Health, but no two of them could Keep Company—the fair Lady also arrived with a Letter from Hetty and Crane. none from Tom. I wish my Letters are not sunk. I suspect the Hand they came thro.

Lawrence made Coll in Cornwallis's. He mistakes our Great Minister—either Comprehends not or willfully. Under pretence of the exchange, He had His power and is supported, but He is unequal to the thing in Every respect was He Honest. Our want of Cash proves it—not a farthing in the Colony and great Complaints[16]—Scott might find out things at Boston had He sense. but people are Affraid of Speaking—or things might be proved as clear as Day light. money expected by Scott.

To Friday. 17th August. the weather continues good—would be very Hot but for the breeze, which makes it excellent weather for fish. No fogs but such as I observe in the Journal. the 16th August Arriv'd a french Sloop sent in by the Tryal from about Canso. had been with Military Stores for D'lutre [Le Loutre] at Sadiack [Shediack], and also four Deserts from Cornwallis Regiment. As Usual I Know nothing of this affair but truely wish all Success to Every undertaking [20 mm.]—whether proper to take this sloop when in peace with France and on the other Hand why not stop Every supply to the Enemy. Sir Danvers dayly expected from Newfoundland. I wish He was arriv'd. Great preparations for the expedition. Rous the fair Lady and several transports[17] saild for the Bay of Fundy.

To Sunday 19th August—the weather clear warm and fine. This day the troops under Lawrence went up in Shallops[18] to Sackville Fort. I went that far with them wishing to go the Whole expedition. would have gone had I not Hopes of going Home this Winter.

To Sunday August 26th—Our Heavy rains fell the begining of this week, with strong Gusts of Wind, this supposed to be the August Storm. the twenty third the Alderney Arrived—I had Letters from My Lord, God bless Him, Tom and poor Hetty &c. A Brigantine enter'd the Harbor with the Alderney in a Gale of wind. went out again next Day. never More heard of. I suspect this done by Order—not time to trade Now—Or on other bussiness for I suspect both.

Sunday 26. Sir Danvers Arrived in the Saltash Sloop of War from Newfoundland. I recd Letters from Lawrence this Day from Camp at Pisequid. a Dirty wet March. the Bowsprits in Distress. expect Rous next Day at Minas to embark for Chignicto.[19] God send them Success. they fall down the River to embark there. fine weather now and they may be embarking at this time. the date of His letter 25th August.

> Sir Danvers told a Story of a Man with Davidson pass at Newfoundland—they are pass'd any where. will his coming be of service to Me? and shall I go &c &c?

they take possession of Chignictou on the English side of the River. fired upon from a Dyke formed into an intrenchment which Lawrence took Sword in Hand. poor Brewse wounded in the Knee.[20] proceed very well.

> poor Bartelo Kill'd in a skirmish. what I always expected would be His fate. by all accounts His Men did not behave well. Howe murdered under a french flag of truce.[21] this act of Barbarity in the french must make them suppose Howe of infinite consequence as done by His Friend L'Corne.

Sep[r] the 4th. Sir Danvers Sailed for Lysbon in the Salt Ash. the America sailed a week before. More Rain this season than fell last Year and we are much More Sickly. Sir Danvers somewhat Affraid of falling ill. Thank God I have my Health, tho' much out of Humour that I could not go to England this winter to see the poor Hettys. God Help them and protect them. I live in Hopes of seeing them the beginning of next summer please God.

thank god that the Governor is now more obliging to me and Every thing very easy Except that I long to see my poor wife and Child. Davidson sail'd for England in the America the later end of Sept[r].[22] I shall never change my opinion of Him I think for He intended Us no good and was most certainly a Jack,[23] countenancing onely such. there is not one in ten of the Clan[24] that is not so inclined—in His menagement of money matters certainly not clever and a Knave into the Bargain I fear. poor Lawrence behaves well and tho' He has His provisions in Plenty and has made a little Kind of fortifications I am in fear for Him this winter both from the Enemy and weather. the season there is much more severe by the indraught of the Bay of Fundy and the Marshes—besides the distance in Lat and firing not to be had without Danger. Also the Enemy may be more powerfull in Winter as travelling over the snow is then most easy, that probably they may bring Cannon upon Him, As it not above ten days march distant from Quebec.[25] God Almighty Protect Lawrence. I am easier in my mind as I endeavour'd to do my Duty consistant with the Love I bear Lawrence by proposing to the Governor to spend my winter with Lawrence and go in the Casco sloop that sail'd from Hence Oct[r] 25th. but the Governor thought proper to order Me Here. poor Gates will do better without Cotterell. He is not yet arrived.

the Kings birthday[26] and the later end of Oct[r]. fine weather tho' we had a fall of snow and some frost about the 20th of Oct[r]. the 31st Oct[r] and Nov[r] the 1st the wind at SE—great falls of rain with fogs.

to Nov[r] 5th—great rain. more than Usual. Wind SE. a very great sea with the Highest tides we have Yet had—Cottrel return'd this day from Chignictou. last from Annapolis after a tedious passage—left Honest Lawrence well and poor Gates—I had a Letter from both. that from Lawrence most Kindly expressive of the Friendship subsisting between

Us—Gates Honest and In Character. this day also the French officer Chambon[27] sail'd with His sixty men for Lewisbourg. I was right I think in advising to suffer the soldiers to carry their Arms. this Brig was taken by Rous convoying a schooner to the River St Johns with provisions for the Indians and thus Armed to fight His Way thro'.[28] the vessel condemn'd in Our Admiralty[29]—certainly right not to suffer Her to go out of our Port nor can a Parole of Honor be taken from such rascals.[30] However I fear this will make a great Noise between the two Courts—Cap^n L- Crass[31] took another in August Last in Bay Verte and she was also condemned. to day Novr 6th the Weather clears up with a light frost and the little wind that is at NW. the two friends[32] are not arriv'd and I greatly long for a Letter from the poor Hetty's. God Bless them.

Novr 11th Sunday—today the weather turn'd very Cold and continued for two days as severe a frost as any we have yet had. the thermometer as low as Ever Known Here—Yet no snow hath fallen except a very little which the Sun melts in the day.

friday Novr 16th. bright and clear with frost and Gentle Wind NW. It is to be Hoped this weather will clear the Air and make the settlement More Healthy. we have had more sickness this fall than last—the Weather Warm and Wet and violent Storms at Sea. by accounts from Chignictou they have secur'd their little Fort against All Attacks, but I fear some Attempts will be made on them this winter. Warburton's people[33] desert greatly, but that will be prevented by the fort. Thank God I have had my Health during all the Illness we have had.

Decr 7th. the Nancy Brig: Stone Master sailed for England. I wrote to My Lord Crane Hetty and Tom. God Bless them all and Grant that we may once More meet again. Lawrence's Letter went to Mr White by the Nancy and I wrote to Him. No sort of news from Lawrence. my best wishes attend Him. We have a random report that forty Indians are on their march towards Us from Cobequid—they May stop a Currier or pick up some straglers but can do nothing More, not even at Dartmouth[34] and this again ought to be consider'd that they have continu'd long in a body at Chignicto without the support expectd from the French, and this is their season for Hunting to support their families, so that may be their errand—

to Dec[r] 14th Friday. the weather continues much milder than last Year. no snow fell, but Sharp frosts and thaws as the wind shifts from NW to SE. a sloop from Annapolis Here, loaded with Cannon thought to be lost tho will be very great as it cannot be soon repair'd. also a provision vessel from New York to Chignictou With Money for the troops there lost on the Seal Islands.[35] but thank God the Colonel [Lawrence] has provisions and Money sufficient for His people till He can be releiv'd, and is in a proper disposition to receive the Enemy.

To Dec[r] 30th. the weather continues extraordinary favourable. Clear sunshine with sharp frost but no snow has fell as Yet, expect [except] on the 27th the wind shifted SE with a violent gale for 12 hours which abated with the strongest shower of rain I ever saw. Cook sail'd Xmas day and this storm would bear hard on Him if He was near Shore—excessive fine weather.

To Sunday Jan[ry] 6th—7th set in for snow.[36] continues to the 8th. very seasonable for we have had no snow this Year—the 7th recd a Letter from Coll Lawrence—Alls well with Him—to Dec[r] 29th with the finest season ever Known. the Date of His Letter the 9th 10th of Jan[ry]. the finest weather Known with about a foot snow on the Ground—the 12th a thaw set in with thick fog, and continu'd till the 16th when it Blows hard and rains violently. Wind SE, so that all the frost and snow is gone. this is greatly unusual by all Accounts and much different from last year. However it has this good Effect as to Keep the communication open between Annapolis and Chignictou—and if the Canada French intended to attack Lawrence at Chignicto by the Help of the snow and frost to bring their Heavy Baggage or Guns if they have any—this will disappoint them. nor have we as yet felt any ill Effects in point of Health Here.

124 Dollars under the Box.[37] took out of the Bag Jan[ry] 4th thirty Dollars. 8th Jan[ry]—took twelve Dollars more. Six Dollars More; eight Dollars more Jan[ry] 16th.—Remains now onely forty in the Box.

Febry 1st 1750—the Governor of Canada's letter arrived.[38] I wish it bodes no ill to Lawrence—it seems to me an excuse onely that He may Attack Him and that He certainly will do if He finds Himself Able. perhaps the weather may have disappointed His schemes. Troops are certainly arrived at Chediac from Lewisbourg but whether cannon is not certain: besides the sloops don't come near enough to the shore to Land them if they have any. this is impudent to send Cannon for we Know Indians can not Use them.

to the 4th of Feb[ry]—scarce any snow on the Ground but Heavy rain often with Gusts of Wind, and as the wind Changes light frosts.

Good News arriv'd from Lawrence Febry 8th by Cobb sent to Annapolis for Wood. Chignictou Garrison in good Health. the Beau Bassin never Known navigable at this time of Year those forty Years past. The French in their old posts very much distress'd for want of Every necessity as nothing can be sent from Canada, this favorable Winter. We want for nothing and the distress of the French even an addition to our strength there.

Saturday 9[th] Febry. Priracy [piracy] sworn against pow[e]r[39]—Every Body for committing Him except my self—I Know his case baleable [bailable]—and think the prosecution malicious—but let Him be try'd by a Jury.

To the 11[th] of Feb[ry]—the finest weather possible. the Wind at NW. light frosts at SE. rain—but no snow falls.

Martin at Boston left in the lurch by M^r D-d-n. if He was
to be examined more truth would come to light. at an
entertainment this minister had from Jeffrey[40] and faction
Curious Healths drunk but not enquired into. Every thing
happens as I ever expected. Lawrence would have been Attack'd but for this favourable winter by the Accounts we
had from Boston by a Prisoner return'd from Quebec. the
Affair of Power is productive of much mischeif and has set
the people in an uproar at Green. He is a Coxcomb at best
but malicious in this prosecution.[41]

Febry 27th—Nesbit[t] behaves ill and is discharged: the
rancour left by Davidson against Green and indeed every
one prompted Him to it—but still this is what Green
almost deserves, for He is haughty in Office without
one amiable Quality—Mauger displeased at Him and
threatens to leave. a general dislike to Green and I fear that
to support Him may bring too great an odium on the Gov-r
&c—talk of petitioning the Governor on this occassion but
this is impertinent. strange stories about Him if true and
that seldom regard'd when passion runs High. Mauger at
the Head of the people. All this foolish enough, for
Government is not to [be] thus frigh[t]n'd: Yet some regard
should be had for the people—

To March 1st. finer weather never Known except sometimes.
about 12 Hours rain or sleet and light frosts at night as the
wind shifts. two fishing schooners arriv'd Feb^ry 27th for
Freeman Gunters[42] supposed to be on the Banks. I think they
are later than last Year, and not so great a preparation for
fishing as might have been expected tho fine season we have
had. We think the winter now gone, as the sap is apparently
up. but some light falls of snow must be expected—

the 2^d of March. a little snow fell today.

the 3^d of march. fine pleasant sunshine. thank God I have my
Health and Grant that my Wife and Child may be well and
that we may Once More meet Again.

fourscore and Seven Dollars—twelve taken out, and three before. thus it stands March 3^d. three and 4 more.

the 4th 5th and 6th of March as cold weather as we have had this year and much snow has fell. Wind NW. a Strong Gale.

I like not the oath pressed last Council[43]—there seems to be a shadow of Guilt there, or suspicion of somebody. I would have opposed it, if I had thought it agreeable to—&c. March 9th this Council Held.

the frost continues as severe as at any time this winter till the March 11th—a thaw set in with fogs and rain and the Ground clear again.

12th. close foggy weather. in expectation hourly of provisions from new york. the Colony in great want of bread &c. Provision Arrives, and the spring Opens with fine weather to March 19th.

tot: 22. rem: 65. M^h 14th.[44]

To March 28th—the finest weather ever Known for the season. March 26th the Indians Attack'd Dartmouth at nine in the Morn: came up to the Brush and fir'd a Platoon. Broke a sentry's thigh with no other Hurt—attempt'd to be pursu'd but in vain—they pick't up two three stragglers—as usual. one poor boy return'd scalp'd[45]—27th a courier brought Letters from Lawrence. all well there except some little discontents among each other. a Lieu[tenant] in Lasscell's[46] throws up His commission—getting all our Warlike sea craft in readyness. much will depend on their activity and proper dispositon. it is time they were at their several Stations Bay Verte and tantamere[47]—else the Enemy will be in possession of Every necessary, warlike stores and provision &c.

the Boston people raise the value of Dollars to six shilling—this onely will carry off all ours unless we raise Ours

Also. then the Boston people have granted a bounty on the fishery, and we must do the like or loose it. I am sorry they are before Hand with Us.

to April 1st—the warmest weather for the season—but a Heavy fall of snow all this day continues till the 4th April. Snowing and freezing at nights—Wind NW—the snow falls with a South East.

the two friends Arriv'd April 2—a Letter from Hetty—thank God they are well. this ship was blown off[48] last Year. to raise a fund for the bounty on fish. a Duty proposed on Rum imported. in my private opinon I am against all Clogs on trade as Yet. particularly this will affect our American Isles, and antigua has already been obliging to us in taking our fish.[49] then to except Our American Isles, the Boston people may dislike and we are almost wholly in their power for necessarys of Every Kind, and this rum their great profit. but all this we would not mind were we strong Enough not to need their assistance, and on this maxim I am against this Duty on Rum at present. besides the Collecting this Duty will be attended with squables that ought to be avoided in this our Infancy—and Our Merchants will pretend this as a Grievance. and the smell of the Cash has always been a strong Inducement to the Common people of England I am sure, and the Americans have been always used to Rum, and they must have it Cheap as in the other Colonies.[50]

to the 10th April. fine weather returns and L. Crass sails with Lutterel for Chig. put in again that night[51]—Wind SE—a fall of snow with rain continues 11th April.

To 19th April. Cold, Raw weather variable with rain and Catching frost. heavy rain this day at Noon and continues. L Crass proceed'd for Chig. 14th.

No Letters from England Even Now 19th April. God Almighty bless my poor wife and Child and that we may once more embrace each other—My Noble Patron Lord Halifax Crane and my poor Brothers. Thank God for My Health.

The Bounty on fish is the great advantadge proposed[52]—but could we have no other fund for this Bounty? would not England Assist in it and another? we may set up stilleries of our Own, but that it will keep the soldiery and people more sober I can never think. the Project is not bad in it self, but I fear the ill Effects of it in our Circumstances—and some of the Cheif advisors would not perhaps be sorry to see us in some little confusion &c—

19[th] April. a Comittee to settle this. I am one, tho' against Even Mooing so as to make any discontent among the people—overruled—then something must be done. an Inland Impost in the excise way rather than proceed by Custom that frigh[t]neth the trader. unless our Am: Isles are exempted from this Custom the Continent give us nothing but drain our money. the Isle's take our fish: except the Isles then let it be a Custom. the Continent will trade with us While we money Maugre[53] all affronts. the Excise as proposed on the Publicans only must be paid by the Common people onely. suppose then they should [mating?]—that would be bad.

I wish I knew what was right in this Case If it must be done, and I am afraid we are gone too far totally to recede. this I never speak of as nothing I say is much Attended to: tho' no one can wish the Settlement Better than I do.

I do not understand why I am not ordered to Register the out Lots North and South—something is meant by it most certainly, but I am easy if it pleases Him.[54] to[o] often I fear lead by the opinion of others: which He never communicates so as to be set right as to bear a wrong tendancy. The thing I fancy is intended to appoint me as Register of the Province, tho' perhaps He may not see it, Morris having often drop't Hints pointing that way. but I depend on my Noble Patron Lord Halifax. God Bless Him. Please God that I may be ordered to go to England this Summer or I fear I shall break my Heart.

Book 6

[26 April to 20 August 1751]

From the close of my Journal which I think ends April 19th to this day April 26th the weather worse than this time last Year. variable with strong winds and much rain; and this detains our ships expected from England. Recd this day a bill from Maugre [Mauger] of twelve pounds sixteen shilling payable to Wentworth[1] at Boston on the Schooner Account. I am much uneasy not to hear from the poor Hetty's, My Lord, Crane and Tom—God Bless them All and Grant that we may once more meet again.

1751 July [April] 26th.
Nothing new since my last, but think the Rum tax does not go on so briskly as I expected—in the Excise way it is now intended and that will bear hard on the Common people only.[2] But if by Duty should this way be ineffectual and the American Isles excepted, we need not fear affronting our continent neighbours while we have a Dollar in our Pocket.

April 29th—the weather clears up and Warm but the 26th at night blew harder than Ever I Knew it at N. so that I feared if Vessels had been on the Coast they might have been drove of[f]. Yet a vessel came in this day and I am still in Hopes of Letters &c. God send good news.

April 29th. Recd of Mr Green four Score dollars on Account of my Salary—

To May the 1st somewhat more moderate but cold for the season, but May day the most soaking rainy day I have seen.

May 3^d. the day I left the poor Hetty's Now two Years past. God Bless them and may we once More meet again.

May 3^d. Drummond[3] return'd from Chignictou. Honest Lawrence writes by Him Date April 18th the Indians

Scalp'd two of His Men, attack the fort &c—but without further success. complains How Hard all this is not to be able to Make any reprisals in this way without force sufficient to drive off their Friends the French, and for that we have not force had we Orders—No Letters from England therefore Know not How to procede. two Men also taken at Annapolis by the St John's Indians the later end of April and pursued to No purpose and Account.

this page escaped my Journal by mistake:

— — — — — — — —

these losses are trifling, but what I dislike most is that the french have not Orders from Europe to draw of[f] their Indians. if any thing is settled about the boundaries by the Commissaries,[4] the French might have news tho' We have not. therefore I fear they have not settled affairs as we Hope for. But I am clear we shall not have a general French War from the Address we saw, from an Antigua News paper, to the King on His speech to Parliament on settling the Spanish Affair. Nothing Here remarkable as I remember but a Sloop put in from Ireland with the small pox on board to the great terror of all our Americans. she came from Ireland with the poor Wretches they call servants to sell and Belongs to Boston. the small pox being on board made Her put in Here. tho' she pretends she has settlers on board Yet has produced no Letters to that or any other purpose. I fear this Same Vessel will be of much Hurt to the settlement, from the dread both English and french have of the small pox. In such cases the Quarentine at Boston is very extraordinary.—Our fishery is far from the forwardness it was this time last Year. I think we are late in proclaiming the Bounty now its order'd. that might have been done, and let the Rum fund take it's Chance, and Even that we can not now recede from.

to the 6th May. still cold for the season. But this day has given me more Joy than I felt since I left England. the Governor promised that I should carry the first dispatches for England, and please God to Grant me my Health, shall once more Embrace my poor wife and Child, My Good Lord, Friend Crane and my Brothers.

May the 6th. Comes of a Skirmish with Indians, about ten of them, at Cape procupine [Porcupine] with ten of Our Rangers. but six of ours run of[f] to their Boat on the first firing. we lost but one Man, Arbuthnot.[5] the officer wounded but got of[f]—And two Indians said to [be] Killed. these Indians are supposed those that took the men from Annapolis, and Our party of Rangers detach'd by Joe Gorham cruseing the Bay of Menas from the Fort there.

Sunday May 12th. Webb[6] arriv'd with onely one Letter from Sir Danvers to the Governor—of money being granted &c but not so general as expected as I perceive. Davidson sent His memoirs also. No Letters for Me to my great disappointment. Grant O God they may be all well. Webb bring[s] account of the death of the Prince of Wales. I am sorry for it.

May 13th. Dartmouth Attacked by a Large party of Indians and do much mischief. near twenty Kill'd and taken Men women and Children. Our Soldiery are constantly drunk there, neglect their Guards or this would not have happened, for we have fourscore men in Governments pay there. when they did turn out they value themselves that they drove the Indians—but the Indians went of[f], as they always do on those occassions. one or two Indians said to be Killed but we find none of them. a Serjeant at one of the Block Houses there let the Indians pass Him and His Men drawn up without firing a Shot, saying His Orders were to defend the Block House. Now if the Block-House had been empty, Indians would never cram themselves into such a post, and thus our regulars often mistake sticking to the flanders discipline.[7]

To May 14th. the weather colder than Usual and the Spring more backward and much rains falls. However it is better for agriculture to have a wet spring, for as it sometimes happens to be very dry in the spring, grain of all Kinds fail and

particularly the Herbage. witness the first spring we came
Here. that Hay was brought from London to Boston.

To May 23^d. the weather as Usual this time of Year. few fish
caught any where. one Letter by foster[8] from Liverpool from
poor Hetty Date Novr last, in great anxiety to Hear from
Here. Recd another from Hetty by a London Ship Date Jan^{ry}
last. thank God that they were All well then and Grant O God
the[y] may continue so. No Letters from My Lord Crane or
Tom, but expect dayly, as My Lord has not wrote to the
Governor—then my fate, as to my return I Hope, will be
happyly determined—It was right to Ask the Governor first
and Every day seems now an Age to me. Please God I shall
sail sometime in June.

May 23^d. I have recd but one twenty pounds onely of my
Salary since my Accounts were made Up for the last
Year.

To May 29th. fine weather. ships arriv'd from London had
letters onely from Her and the little Girl. thank God they are
both Well, and my Friends, tho' I had not Letters from them.
Yet Hope My Lord has Hinted my return to the Governor.
Clouds gathering apace. certainly a body of Indians in the
province. threaten the Inhabitants if they assist us in the least.
they send Deputies to Complain and beg our patience with
them. received civily but peremptorily ordered to Attend our
Call as Subjects tho' thro the hazard of their lives and to support this send a party of a Hundred regulars and voluntiers to
Pisiquid and Minas—those with troops drawn out of the
Forts may make a good stand, drive off the Indians and so
bring the inhabitants to reason. a very few will guard forts for
Indians will never shut themselves up in one tho' deserted. the
danger is least Jonquier [Jonquière] has sent french among
them in disguise,[9] but they can be but a few and to attack a
fort Indians would never dare if a body of Men takes the
feild—when they fire at a fort they are at sufficient distance
except in the Night. therefore fear not troops in a fort, as they
are sure they will not sally and pursue them, which if the[y]

did the Indians would certainly withdraw—except perhaps leave a small Ambush, and that they would not execute without apparent advantadge. Please God I shall sail with Gorham to Carry Home this Intelligence &c &c.

29th May. certain intelligence that the French have detained several vessels at Lewisbourg. As it certainly is by way of reprisal they have orders from old France—now we hear nothing what our people say about the prizes Rouse and L' Crass took last Year, or How the Limits are to be settled but the Commissarys remain still in France. I think no danger of an Open french War that would quite Hurt. this Clandestine War does us sufficient Damage. the people are more dispirited than they were this time last Year. I wish some of our conceited Gentry do not inspire them with this, but be it as it will something must be done to Keep up their Spirits—I think I can perceive our Regulars much off their Mettle. Proctor when He returns with His now ranging Company must do something to Keep at least the people in the town from fear, but He will be long a coming to picket in the Narrows would give these people ease of Mind and for that reason think it should be done directly. the Lewisbourg people would never venture to detain the Boston vessel but that Know them such dogs that they will do any thing for Money. for Suppose the Boston and all our Colonies were combined never more to trade with them. they must be starved at Lewisbourg. So to Me the French seem in Earnest to venture such a Risque, as I still suppose them not determined on a General War.

The Journey and Masacre the Indians made at Dartmouth was executed in five Days, so that they have a very quick water Carriage which Lewis[10] has discovered. I hope it will turn to advantage. I brought Lewis into Play.[11]

to June the 4th—seasonable weather with Showers of rain &c. today the night summer fog is in the Harbor for the first time. Greens Court of admiralty proceed I think very injudiciously so as to Harbour trade. tho' we have no professed searchers in our Port, Informers are encouraged by Monk and others, souse[12] a ship in their court and seldom fail finding matter sufficient to condemn Her. I am told for Certain that our neighbouring provinces Even Boston make not more seizures. connived at and perhaps it may be proper Here. the severity of penal Laws is never strictly executed—nor intended—but this we are made to beleive with affected caution as to oaths &c. Powers Case is an excellent instance in this point.[13] I forgot this Ships name but she brought Mr Porter[14] Here. She is a Brig from Ireland—with provisions for Saul and a few Settlers.[15] their plea is that these counter band Goods were for these poor settlers.

June 4th 1751. Recd then of Mr Green twenty pounds on Account. Wrote to the Governor to beg leave of absence but he has not spoke to me since and seems displeased but has set on Gates to talk to me—Now I can not stay. the Health, perhaps the life of my poor wife depends on my return and for that reason fear for my self If the Governor should detain Me. God forbid He should, for the Countenance of no Man can ballance the anxiety I should feel if detained Here. It is of consequence that I shall hazzard all on point. It is peevish to detain me when He Knows of How little Use I am rendered, not Suffered to Act in any thing—scared to think on any subject, I mean Aloud, and when I attempt it, not attended to but much disliked as forwards &c &c. I am so vexed with this uncertainty about going that I am far from Well. violent vomiting and purging.

to June 13th. weather seasonable &c &c but Kept in Hot water by Indians at Dartmouth. constant Alarms, but come to action. Lewis is on that side with a Party. What I fear is for our Suburbs. the Alarms on the Other side perhaps intended to draw of[f] our force the more securely to attack them Here. the narrows is not secur'd but snubed when I spoke of it. Rouse saild for Chignictou. Our Army Politicians as bad as with Lawrence at Chig. but they dare not talk of it with the same boldness. Yet it strikes a damp on All the peoples Spirits, tho' we in town Here are safe enough, and with a Picket or Guard at the Narrows as I observed before we might have as much Ground as we could cultivate and be in Absolute security.

Our party return'd from Minas and Pisiquid. brought the Deputies—they promise fair and seem to know now that the drift of the French is to harrass them so with Indians and perswasitions to quit the Province. tho' they hate Us the[y] care not to leave their native Country.

Clearly proved by the mate that informed, that He was instigated to it by Monk. the Whole court attempt to clear themselves [in the Power case] from any such Imputation, but fear they will be little credited.

To June 18th. Hot weather with fogs as usual. two poor wretches hanged to day. the Lord have mercy on their souls. Please God I am determined to return with Gorham. the Governor has consented, but with some reluctance, Yet why this reluctance Is matter of Wonder with Me[16] as never consulted, I mean in private, or any Occassion: the bussiness of the Office He attends solely to Collier about, as if I Know nothing of the Matter and Even in that the office bussiness is much curtailed, for we have not the out Lots to register, and Why I Know not, as it certainly belongs to Our Office. a small action at Chignictou about this time in which we rather had the better for we lost not a Man and the Enemy supposed to loose 3 and one of 'em of consequence.If the Ambuscade had taken place we might have given a good Account of the Enemy. Lutterel is Gallant. I wish His Spirits may not carry Him too far. I am still of opinon that if we loose any capital action, it will affect the Cause more than the mear [mere] loss of the Men. therefore every risque to be avoided. I wish Lawrence was return'd. I have much to say to Him.

June 19th. Gorham tricked me about sailing but go please God I will, and Grant that my Wife and Child may be well. What should I stay for, when supposed uncapable of any thing or treated as such? and Why a seeming Unwillingness to suffer me to go Is Strange. this Unwillingness in Him with the fear of not going Almost distracts me. so far am I distracted about it that I have been really very ill, but bled, which Assisted me, and I am thank God June 21st much better. Several things in this Colony if attended to might be of service. for Instance Now we are glutted with live stock both from Our French and Sister Colonies, we might have places to Keep them, Cornwallis Isle, but if it was picketted at the Narrows in one Years time Even in this Article it would pay it self. then the security to the inhabitants. agriculture would go on with spirit whereas Now we are Obliged to Keep a Guard at the North End of the town. the Expence of that will be little Short of the other and should the Indians appear on this our little peninsula it would distress us greatly. Then again Grain is very cheap Here at times—as Cheap as at Boston, but then that depends on the Navigation, which at other times makes it excessive Dear. now the Boston people have public Graineries under proper regulations and this we ought to imitate—which I have spoke of, but not attended to as usual. Boston grows not the grain they consume but have it from Connecticut Rhode Island and even Philadelphia, yet by these Graineries they menage so that it never comes to an exorbitant Price.

I am far from well. My Spirits are in such a constant Hurry about my return. Grant me my Health O God and prolong my Days once more to Embrace my poor wife and Child My Lord Halifax my Friend Crane and my poor Brothers. Protect them all O God.

to June 21st. weather seasonable. much fish brought in tho' fewer Employed. on the 20th the first Mackarel for the season. this day L' Crass with Rogers sailed for Bay Verte. High time I am sure. L' Crass was delitory in the Affair when the Order Came and I think the Order came to[o] late considering the importance of Bay Verte. the Enemy have certainly some Cannon at Chignictou by fireing a shivel [swivel?] at our people from the Block House. A Supply of Cannon will demolish us there. this Day Lord Colvil from Boston. What His bussiness may be I can not tell. He behaved strangely last time.[17] and Mr Bastide from Annapolis with a tribe of

Engineers &c. their Account is that a French Ship of War of thirty tons is in the River St. Johns. strange News if this be true and the consequences may be bad, Rouse being in the Bay of Fundy with Orders to vissit the River St Johns. they may fall foul of each other.

To July Monday 1st 1751—the weather as usual with fogs, but I think rather more rain than last year. two days past Lord Colvil sailed for the Bay of Fundy. Rouse, Dove[18] and Him may surely menage the French Ship if they meet with Her. I am still of Opinion she comes from Canada and not old France as She gives out and perhaps it may be all a Story, Tho it looks strange not to hear any thing from Rouse by the last Couriers. He may have stretch'd up to Chig. without calling at Annapolis and so we hear nothing of Him.

July 4th. preparing Every thing for my Voyage in the Osborne. but Couriers from Minas arrive and tell Us that Lawrence was gone for Annapolis in Rouse and was to sail immediately for this place. fresh Orders then from the Governor that the Osborn was not to sail till they arrive. tho' I want to see Lawrence Every delay Hurts my very soul. they have got Cannon at Chig. what I always feared by way of Bay Verte. this will Keep our poor people in Hot Water, and I wish it may be no worse.

To July 6th—More foggy than usual and a fall of Most violent Rain—much fish damaged.

to July 12. clears up after the Rain and excessive hot weather. the begining of July Bastide sailed for newfoundland and the Cornwallis with a Packet for England. this seems hard that I had not that Honor to carry it.

it is now July 12 and no Rouse Arrived.[19] a Ship with Palatines arriv'd yesterday from Amsterdam.[20] No News from poor Hetty. Grant O God that they may be all well: Palatines set to Picket Dartmouth. a very good work, but Green had private Ends in it. if the Narrows were also picketed it would be well. Snubbed again when I proposed it. An Impost on the Entry of continent Rum. this I proposed before but not attended to for that reason. Yet All this I care not should I go Home.

Sunday 14th. hard News. Rouse with Lawrence on board Sprang his Main Mast at Annapolis. God Help me, what ill luck this to be thus detained Again yet Grant me O God a Happy meeting with My little family and Friends.

To the 19th. No Rouse Yet and Every day an age to Me. so far it Hurts me that I pray to God for ye Continuance of my Health and to support me. Vessels dayly Arrive but not A Letter from Poor Hetty—she certainly thinks me on my Voyage and the disappointment May crudley Hurt Her and that is my Great Grievance—Yet please God we may Happyly once More meet Again. Clear weather returns at Starts—Yet More rain falls than we have as yet had this time of the year.

Late in July[21] Lawrence arrives with Rous to my Great Joy. two ships are arriv'd with Palatines—one company fix'd at Dartmouth to picket, the other at Strasburghers road on our little peninsula. This is right and gives great Joy to the people. I am glad it is done—tho' when I proposed it snubbed for My pains. Here is an Absolute security for us now and people will go about their improvements Chearfully. It would really not have been of any great detriment should we have lost 4 or 5 people but the disgrace would have been great and the terror Greater and so would have Hurt us.

a bounty granted of ten shilling p ton on building any Craft. every right [wright?] and many vessels are now contracted for.[22]

the Germans at Gorhams point teazing the Governor to settle at pisequid. the thing right in it self, but our french seem now in better Humor than Usual and if these people go Now they may take umbrage at it, as encroaching on their property—the old French people ready enough to perswade them to it. the Indians at Chignictou behave very unintelligible in venturing into Our fort, when it is supposed they do not mean a real peace, and yet they could see nothing there that could encourage them to continue the War. However Lutterel behaved well in not Hurting them.

L' Cras is a Coxcomb to return from His station before His time with His terrible Account of His French Fleet at Lewisbourg.[23] the News now is that this fleet is not so terrible as He sets forth in His Journal. it was odd enough that a Large french ship should hover so long about our Cape Sambro', and hard that we have no Ship of force to Speak to her.[24]

To August Saturday the 3^d. in immense anxiety of Mind about my Voyage and this day Please God came on board about one at Noon. could get no further than Georges Island. there cast anchor. Rains and Fogs continue more than Usual. Grant me O God a Safe and Happy Voyage with Health, once More to Embrace My poor Wife and Child My Noble Patron My Friend Crane My poor Brothers and Sir Lynch.

Sunday August 4th. very little wind. anchor'd under Mauger beach. Collier Rickson[25] and Porter came on board us in My Schooner.

Monday 5. ten in the Morn. weighing our Anchor. little or No wind.

God Grant Us a Good Voyage. we hope to leave the land to day Monday August 5th.
We sail'd with an ease Gale this day.[26]

To Wensday 7th. easy Gales and fine clear weather. an observation taken told that we are clear of Isle Sable—I wish they understand these affairs. at six this Evening a Calm—we have seen Wales of all sorts and Gorham explains to Me their particular distinctions—God Grant me a Happy meeting with my poor wife and Hetty, my Patron the Peer, my Friend Crane my poor Brothers and Sir Lynch.

to Saturday August 10th. the clearest weather Ever Known almost, in those seas—but the wind keeps to a point in the East so that we can not make our Course. Gorham killed a Porpoise in Whaleing manner and I am sure He must be dextrous at it. We have a leak in Our Vessel that requires pumping Ever[y] two Hours which gives me much uneasyness—but Am told there is no danger in it. I trust to the Almighty who hath hitherto preserved Me, that I shall be once more Happy in the Embraces of my poor Wife Child and Friends. God Grant us a Good Voyage.

> Saturday August 10th. those Easterly Winds and Clear must certainly bring our shipping into Halifax or the Governor will be very unhappy. Surely He will not think of sending the Swiss[27] up into the Country at this time; for, if there be any truth in those French inhabitants, those seem now inclinable to be well with Us—and this will certainly disoblige 'em in point of property. besides now we picket in the istmus there will be room enough in safety. All this I have told Lawrence to represent to the Governor. as to my self I am not allowed the priviledge of a serious conversation with Him and when I offer any thing in the rank I bear, rejected for that reason, tho afterwards taken up.

To Wensday 14th. continues clear but very squaly, as hard gales as Ever I Knew at sea except one day in the Sphinx, and we leak so much the sailors grumble of pumping—and this is no small uneasyness but please God—He will preserve us All. this day 14th the weather moderates thank God. Yet with a breeze at East and by North directly opposite to Our Course—and this wind hath continued in this point ever since we have been Out—please God we shall now have a favorable wind, it seldom happening to continue So long in the Eastern point. Our leak also is more favorable to us—supposed to be on the starboard tack and we lie now on the larboard. When the Wind favors Us I hope Gorham will be prevailed on to put into some port in newfoundland. God Send Us a Good Voyage. We are Now in or About the Latitude 40. see flying fish and Dolphins.

Recd of Mr Green twenty pounds about three days before I sailed on this voyage, the onely sum I have recd from Him since my Accounts we last made up—to Christmas last as I remember but that will appear by the Accounts themselves. I write this Wensday August 14th 1751.

August thursday 15th—the wind came a point westerly. very favorable for Us and continued till Monday 26th in which time we made good Way, Our Easting being now about two hundred and fifty leagues from the Lizard.[28] and now it hath pleased God that the wind is come to an East point much Against Us. but Grant O God that it may Alter so that we may make Our passage—it is now exactly three weeks since we left Halifax. thank God the leak does not increase Upon Us—and the first land we can now Hope for Is England.

Monday 26th August. I have a head ach torments me much but the Almighty I Hope will be pleased to restore me to My Health. We met the Gosport near the banks of New-foundland and not Enquiring whether any body that Knew me was on board hath left strange impressions upon Me least My Dear Hetty might be there. I do what I can to perswade my self of all most the impossibility of it—or it would affect me greatly. Grant O God that we may once More meet Again.

Book 7

[20 May 1752 to 12 April 1753]

May 20th Wensday 1752. Left My poor Wife and Child in Charles Street St. James's Square. God Almighty Bless and preserve them, and Protect them, and Grant O God that we may once More meet again. I trust In the Almighty that we Shall. Got to Lyphook[1] that night.

Thursday 21st. at Portsmouth at Noon. Friday and Saturday at Portsmouth. contrary Wind.

Sunday 24. went on board the Jason Spithead. can not Sail. wait On Colonel Hopson At Fareham[2] in the Afternoon.

Monday 25th. at Eight forenoon on board the Jason weighing Anchor to Sail—God Almighty Grant Us a Good Voyage.

Friday May 29th. No happy day to me. got to Plymouth. Write to Hetty onely. Governors Ditto &c.

This a long passage. Bought two pipes[3] of Wine of[f] Catanach at Medeira, Value forty two pounds, and sent bills of Exchange to Tom for that sum Dated July 8th New Style.[4] Wrote to Poor Hetty and Him from thence with a promise to be sent by the first conveyance to England. God Bless my poor Dear Wife and Child and Grant we may Once More meet again.

Simple Enough but the Man of the Ship[5] has taken offence at me. would certainly have quitted the Ship at Medeira and gone in a Snow to New York and so made my passage, but that M[r] Hopson Hinted to me the Contrary, and it was right in such point to take His Advice. This Cap[t] I despise so much that He can neither give me offence nor do me Honor. So I am easy on that Head.[6]

Sailed From Portsmouth May 25th 1752.
Arrived at Plymouth May 29th.
Sailed From Plymouth June 7th 1752.
Arrived at Madeira June 23[d].
Sailed From Madeira June 28th.
Arrived at Halifax Nova Scotia On Sunday July 26th 1752—[7] Thank God for My Health and good Passage and Grant O God that My poor Wife and Child may be well and that we may Once More meet again.

Since I came Here, attend to the Stange Humours of the people and perceive them forming foolish little divisions among themselves. I Enter into none of them and am determined to continue thus. Therefore circumscribed much in my Chat, which gives me no pain, as I am in no Spirits, tho thank God in very Good Health. M[r] Cornwallis more than Commonly Civil. M[r] Hopson the Man I expected Him to be. An Enquiry Ordered into M[r] Littles conduct.[8] I am of the Committee much against my will—Knowing this man greatly to have In-jured the Public, and I hate the Fatigue and Nonsense of Defensive Altercations. Wrote to My Lord and Hetty August 8th and again August twenty fifth. this Committee will Keep us sitting every Day perhaps for this fortnight to come, and not possible to detect half the wickedness of the Deeds of those concerned in the stores, which they would never have ventured upon without the connection of M[r] Townsend[9] and Kilby[10] at Home, on Whose interest they Depend by the Means of [Benjamin] Gerrish, Townsends Agent, into Whose Hands it is apparent they Threw much Profit at the Risque of the Settlement and to distress M[r] Cor[n]wallis. the seed of all this was sowed by Davidson. However this En-quiry will clear M[r] Cornwallis and make His Choice of Saul very Proper.[11] This I have wrote to My Lord Now and told Him of it in England.

If I am not very much ill treated in my Office and other Af-fairs I hope to out live the Winter Here and Get Home in the Spring, which I would not do on any consideration but that I think it is pleasing to My Lord to Get Home in the Spring. please God I am determined on.

To day August 27th. All the Germans from M[r] Dick[12] Ar-rived Yesterday,[13] and today the Jason Sail'd. a Good rid-dance of that Fool[14] and Jack Allen.[15]

about august 27th Col. Monckton marched for Chignic-tou—will do well enough I Hope.

the three penny scheme laid aside,[16] certainly impracticable in an out settlement but Here I have my Doubts especially in Summer. It had been well if we had gone thro' the Affair of an out settlement for the Germans. want of provisions &c was the Argument against it, for it gives the Germans grounds to Grumble and I fear they will be very troublesome this winter. there appears some seeds of Mutiny among them. fellows desert Every day to Lewisburg and the trade of running away with small Craft very much practised. the French at Lewisbourg boast of their acquisitons in this way, and I fear they have some of their private Friends among us to Corrupt the people. A letter sent from St Johns Isle to encourage our French Inhabitants to quit the province, Yet this they will not do I beleive, at least the major part of them. terms in this Letter doubtfull whether the limits are settled or not. that the Limits are not settled I beleive. Yet it is apparent by the Letter, that they give up all hopes of the Country. this Letter sent to M[auger?]. why not to the [Colonel?].

take up not a farthing of money from Green. Borrowed forty pounds from Saul and sent Bills on Tom to pay it to Mr Baker[17] at London. this Money was part of it to repay Mr Hopson for a Pipe of Madeira. I am entered into the Mess at Station. this I fancy will not Hold Long. [30 mm.] will go and Gates too Giddy.

Sad poor doings, but I like it better than foolish obligations to any such. Cotterell shineing—nothing to me nor can He ever Hold it.[18] If winter was Over then Adeiu to them all for Ever. Cotterell will be hurt if He meddles with Dick in money matters. He is composed of nothing but Prate and Stuff, unable to go thro' any Bussiness—the Whole Bussiness of His office is done by Hinchelwood, and this same Hinchelwood the Impudent sorry fellow I ever took Him to be, Known to tell about town Every transaction in the office, and I suspect further from His Pryeing into Every Affair with the total command of Cotterell, and He will say any thing to Gratify His Own Vanity.

An Act for the releif of insolvent Debtors drawn up.[19] I have no Hand in it, and Doubt the Utility of it. this I Know, it disobliges several Tho' Mauger seems resolved never to be pleased. very foolish in Him, and talks like a fool of things He understands Not. at the Head of all Petitions, and Grumbling ones multiply greatly—from the Germans—wherein they complain of not being sent into an out settlement and all those things grow worse in winter. I wish an out settlement had been formed. I think it might, but we proceed with much Gravity, tho' in the Affair of money and provision Dash away as much as Ever Cornwallis did, and without an out settlement what pretect [pretext] can be made at Home for victualling the last

Years Germans? Yet most of them will perish if they have no provisions this winter. then Again whenever they do go to an out settlement further provisions must be Given them, and this will cause Grumblings at Home I am sure. of all this I am clear as I have a Hand in nothing, and it is Stuff to talk.

Sepr 1st. my Birth Day. Grant O God that we may once more meet again, that my poor wife and Child may be well and all things well with them.

Sepr 3^d alias 14th[20]—Mr Kilby's Brig. arrived with the money. brought Letters from the Poor Hettys & Tom. thank God that they are well. Baptist Cope the Indian Arrived with a proposal for a Peace with His part of the Mickmack Tribe.[21] Assented to with many Forms. Forms not so absolutely necessary if the People are in Earnest as I think they are Now. the St. Johns Indians under a sesation [cessation] of arms but no peace confirm'd with them. talk of their coming Here with Dove. An Out settlement I Know to be the sense of the people at Home. why therefore not attempted tho' the risque is great and that they Know not. My Abstract of the Admiralty Laws certainly lost—it may be kept by the Re[giste]r.[22] I like Him not. My Hound Bitch came.

Sep^{r}17th NS. Mr Little makes Every Delay in His Affairs, so that it is apparent that He intends to Stave it off till Mr Cornwallis is gone, seeing the Use Mr Cornwallis will make of it in England. Nothing more apparent but that he has robbed the Public, tho' for more than the first Half Year Davidson had the sole direction—and when Plunged[23] so that He could go no further threw it into Little's Hands. Still reckning with Mr Townsend by the Gross and not by certificate of the number of settlers victualled.

Sepr 20th. about this time much desertion among the Swiss and Germans—fear more as a Young french Man is come from Lewisbourg In with Zouberbulah[24] that may corrupt these people—and this Zouberbulah Knows Every thing from Hinchelwood. these people yet I believe the folk I took them for. the excuse the Frenchman has for being Here is receiving the Ransom for the schooners taken by the Indians, and indeed at a High rate above half the Value, notwithstanding the Civil Letter wrote to Our Governor by ye Governor of Lewisbourg. the pretence of our foreingners still is the want of being settled in an Open Country.

Sepr 25th. Monday at Council. Orders to Saul to victuall for fifteen Months[25]—No regard to the sixpence &c—these affairs and all others go Home in full with Mr Cornwallis. I touch onely the Orders, whether or not attended to. Starve we must not. the Insolvent Bill I can by no Means like tho' I shall never speak to it—they are wedded to it, and it signifies nothing—will onely propose this to suspend it till we hear the reception it meets with at Home from Mr Cornwallis's representation.[26] I think it big with Evils, as it will hurt our Credit with our neighbours and our Own little private credit Here and it is most certain that on Credit Onely We Live. we run to[o] much on Law making and are unequal to the task——food onely for Law and wrangling.

Octr 21st Saturday. Mr Cornwallis sailed. I wish Him well with All my Heart. much superior to King Log[27] and yet He will spend them as much money. I am out of the Vortex of Dullness[28]—Dind at Sauls and House at Bryans.[29] I beleive the Indians will in some measure come In. We ought not to be niggardly on that Head, tho' we should be Deceived. I can not Hope now to go to Minas and thereabouts to see the mines but certainly they are considerable—on that Head I have wrote &c—In spring, please God I live and am Able, will return to My poor Wife and Child. God Almighty Protect them and that we may Once More Embrace Each other Never to part Again.

For that fool Green to pretend to Law making and His wife making Custards and putting in a Word in favor of some Presbyterian Neighbour. He wants not onely Sense but is the Most partial Rascal Living. Mr Secretary Cotterel much the greatest fool that subsist[s] and yet this fool is a Politian[30] in His way. Made a Councellor.

Octr. 23^d 1752—Duport[31] Order'd secretary to the Council with a Salary £100 p An:[32] All this to sneer the Board of trade— Why does Green still Hold All His Lucrative Employments?

On tuesday Octr 24th an order came to Collier by Hinchelwood to bid Him make out a Deputation in my Name to go by the Couriers that Instant. Mr Collier answer'd it was impossible in point of time—and this deputation was to empower Mr Hamilton[33] to Collect the Droits du Roy in the several Districts Naming them. the Wensday following it came to my Knowledge that such a Demand was made, Which I considered of in this Manner, that a Deputation by Order of Government might for Ever exclude the Receiver from Every thing but a nominal Right, that it might be struck into a president [precedent] and that all Emoluments when any such might Accrue would belong to the Deputee by the Government, and those Emoluments I have been taught to believe might be considerable In time. Further not a word of all this was mentioned to Me by the Governor, as if by No Means concerned in the Affair. this I thought very remarkable as principal ough[t] to be spoke to at least—and of this I told Col: Lawrence very freely and with some astonishment (but the usual Prate prevailed with Him) that I hav[e] not been so much as spoke to on the Affair by the Governor—nor did the Governor send for me till the Saturday Morn: following,[34] when I had prepared a Letter and brought it my self as the whole of my reasoning on the subject, for by this time I found by Lawrence and others that Affair was very serious. I have not a Coppy of the Letter but will Endeavour to make it out from rough Draught. They have all play'd me false in this affair and I shall never trust any of them. they are such Changeable fools. tomorrow at nine I am ordered again before the Governor, but Governors I Know never forgive the least Shadow of contradiction which I have not done, but asserting a Right Even in the modest way amounts to the same thing.

Sunday 29th Oct^r—God Bless my Poor Wife and Child and that we may Once more meet again: Every thing is done by Log to distress me since I wrote Him that Letter. His taking no notice of me is what I care not a Rash for—but He encourages Cotterel to encroach on My Office. I will never dispute any thing with Log Here but have told My Lord. I certainly ought to have the swearing the Grantees and the sealing of the Grants—and Every thing relative to the Grants of Lands—but they are now executed one-ly in the Secretarys office of which He certainly has not the least right. He has never said a Word to me about the office of Register, as if I was no such man nor indeed on any Occasion for three weeks past, and when He speaks matters indifferent.

We have perfected a foolish peice of formality with Major Cope the Indian. Formality is the thing onely thought of. Our Log has not the spirit to Know Essentials, but this compact with the Indian may stand, but not to be Ascribed to any cunning of Ours—except to Pigot[35] who did the whole[36]—and at the completion of it Log would have spoiled all out of a foolish Covetuousness and simple—the most simple for-malities—but we have victualled seventy Indians in Nov^r.[37] why then could not we have victualled the Germans when they were to have inhabited the very same place; and that was the main exception against cantoning them out this winter? Now we Know they have deserted and are well recd at Lewisbourg, write to their Friends to follow them—so we Know not where this will End. this History Mauger gave us—so His trade is apparently at Lewisbourg. His still must be supplied with Molasses—this History I sent My Lord &c by Armstrong.[38]

Now our fools Head are turn'd towards Law making and by Greens advice Every thing is proposed and attended to. this fellow is of All others the most unfit for this End, as having neither common Literature, nor the Knowledge of Man-kind, and what is still worse, the most Corrupt Heart, selfish and rational to the last degree, unsatiable in the Lust of Obedience—Yet not without the old Fanatic Mask, tend-ing alway in his ordinances to trample such as pay Him not sufficient Homage or to gratifie such as do, and did I not push on Collier to form His Crudities into words it should be shamefull to read them. Yet this fool is all in all and always will be so, for Log can never distinguish.

In Decr. 14th Cooks insolence and imprudence brought against Him an Action for Granting a warrant, tho' out of the Commission of the Peace. in defending this, His impudence was so great as to affront the Bench, for which He was mulcked[39] twenty pounds. but Cook with His usual swaggerings threatned the Justices and declared He was still in Commission, moved for an Arrest of Judgement &c to clear up this. a tryal by presentment of the Grand Jury was brought on, and Cook had a verdict thro' proper means. But not satisfied with this Cook makes a party—and impeaches the Justices—and this is to be brought on before the Governor and Council on New Years day. Wonderfull that the people should be of Cooks party, and yet all of them despise the Man, and this the Colonel[40] is at the Head of, calling it persecution in the Justices. Now the Bench are of New england influenced by Green—and this Green is propounding penal Laws for those His tools to work with; and yet this Green at this time will lurch[41] the Justices and take His Head out of the Collar. that a stop should be put to Green is right, but these poor Devils the Justices suffer, and Every Attack upon them by way of petition from the people is lopping of[f] much Authority from Government, and this Log can never see.

It is now the 30th of Dece^r—thank God my stay will not be long Here Now. God Bless my poor Wife and Child. Abundance of our Foreigner[s] are deserted to Lewisbourg and invite their Friends after them. this we Know from Mauger whose trade to Lewisbourg is now apparent to support His Still. Wrote to My Lord Tom and poor Hetty by Armstrong. early in Decer. recd two Letters from Hetty, Date Combermere[42] August one, the other 18th Sepr. Thank God she did not Hurt Herself with Her fall and that they are both well. Jan^{ry} 3 1753. Yesterday those Letters came to Hand.

Jan^{ry} 3^d 1753—this mighty accusation against the Justices was opened in public at the Court House, in much form, for Form we attempt at but can scarce arrive at what is right even in Form. [Tease?] I am sure we never shall or ought to have put a stop to this before now. Corny [Cornwallis] would I am sure—as it is no One can tell where it will stop. please God I go Home in April at furthest, and my sense of the whole I will not put down in writing.

On Jan^{ry} 10th recd Dear Hettys packet from Doctors Commons.⁴³ Date 14th Octr. Thank God that they were then both Well and Grant O God that they may continue So—On the twenty'th of Jan^{ry} at Night I had a most dismal Dream that my Dear Life was Dead, and I have not been easy since. Protect and preserve them both O God that we may once more meet again. I receive no Letters but from them. It is now the twenty second of Jan^{ry}, and please God I will make what haste I can to My Dear Love.

—a very easy Winter. as yet no snow on the Ground. If we do any thing put the Ax to the root, repeal the Law that makes this place a Kind of an Asylum for All Vagabonds⁴⁴ in screening them from all prior debts to their arrival Here. then your Greens will with draw, and the rest of His Gang, to wallow Here in Luxury pride and affected Honesty, even Insolent Power, defrauding the Just Creditor. and this Is the Case with Green and Most of them. this will do, and the proposal Honest. but to attend to the Cabals of the people—there is no End of it. it weakens the Hands of Goverment—not that I infer that the Goverment is in weak Hands.

It is wonderfull How steadyly foolish we go On. It is now the twenty-third of Jan^{ry}. still Hearing this Idle complaints of the Merchants as they call themselves, when they make nothing out against the Justices's. We are very weak thus to Induldge them. the next point will be to fly at us. Attempted Collier already, talk of the Laws enacted as foolish and will petition when this is Over. Mauger and Grant⁴⁵ at the Head of all this. this Green never does propose any thing but with a proud selfish End either to distress such as pay Him not Homage or to Oblige those that do. to take the five Acre Lots from the people if this do not clear them in such a time because it is impossible they should as thus circumstanced and this is Greens doings, to throw this property into the Hands of Newengland Men. Not that such of them as are Here have greater Ability than Our English, but they are supplied from Newengland and work for the people there. If it was but the base clearing of the ground it is truely equal to us How or by Whom it is done—but Here is a Manifest tendency to get the Whole of the property and the power into their own Hands: but We ought to rectifie this and not suffer such insolencies on Government. but when a Man is Obstinate Dull and fearfull then Cabals and Factions take place and Anarchy will ensue. before I leave the Colony I will endeavour to repeal the Assylum Law. this I fear I can not compas[s], for their is ever a Kind of Sympathy between Dull Spirits. I am not the least taken Notice of nor Care I, and Every encroachment made on My Office and that is a Matter of indifference as I have sent My Lord an Account of the Whole, except with my intention to endeavor at the repeal of the Assylum Law—and that will lay the Ax to the root If I succeed. but I have no Assistance, not one I can trust—the Col. as always trimming[46] tho' an Honest man I beleive.

to day is the 30th Jan^{ry}. Still going on with the same foolish Affair of the Merchants. they had the assurance to day to Attempt to cros[s] examine Me, which I refused to comply with, as I thought it became me. I expect a further Attack from them, for there is no end of their folly and Insolence; and this any body might have seen at first, if they could see. truely Now the Man is somewhat satisfied; but when this trouble is over, these very people again will be looked upon As the standing Oracles notwithstanding, for the High Priest directs All and these people are His cou[n]sellors—Your Grants and Magees etc. Mauger and Saul onely the Heavy weights that gives them Motion. How Cornwallis would have laughed at All this. certainly as Yet the most gentle winter Ever Known in this Country. God Bless my Wife and Child; please God I will leave them and their Laws soon, (for a Dog would not live Here sensible of the total folly of the Whole) and return to my Dear Love—and May the Almighty Protect You both. I hope for my departure from Hence about the Middle of April, and, with the Protection of the Almighty, Hope to see you All Well in England.

Febry 16th. 1753— to day the first fall of snow, as Customary to this Country, We have had this Year. the Priest[47] seems to have the Ear. At the same time certainly foolish in Him to be encouraging those Male contents, Grant Mauger and Magee; it is to be accounted for onely as they dislike Cornwallis—but this surely can never be true prudence, for they will also distress this Man—If He will not distress all the people they Hate. And the bussiness of Goverment can never go on If they are always to be Humored. Grant most certainly intends what Hurt He can to the Colony. Mauger cares not what becomes of it, so that He can get money by the distillery, and run[n]ing Rum from Lewisbourg. a proud troublesome sorry Rascal this Mauger Is, presuming on His great se[r]vices to the Colony when it is but to Serve Himself, and we might Have twenty in Equal circumstances with Him did we give them Equal encouragement, and it is the utmost folly to give way to His insolencies, when they are not to be satisfied.

Our poor Big Man hath onely the appearances of what He ought to be and the encouraging these people is intend'd as a Sly reflection on Cornwallis and to gain popularity, As He and His foolish Priest think. But they will be deceived. I can foresee much confusion as the result of these Paltry Politics, M[r] Secretary Coxcomb as He is. this big Man still attends to His simple Prate—the Colonel with all His science of Argumentation is not the Minister neither—they are All such fooles, Jealous of each other, that so little state was Ever half so ridiculous—so unable to do any thing had they any Body to contest with. But the Justices are so poor and so dependant they dare not squeak whatever Injury is offered them. Morris would Else work the Haughty Mauger and His

Clan. Something so weak in Goverment to give way to these wrangles—and gravely to Attend to them—as Must have made them dispicable to Each party. Not but that the Justices are Rascals—but then they are Rascals in Authority, and if You give up authority, the next Insult will be at Your self. Certainly such a set of Block Heads never Joyn'd Loggerhead before—the impudent Pert Prying Priest, the Coxcomb Secretary, and the conciliating Collonel. but that Mauger has no Sense And the Rest poor. they would play the Devil Else with them.

As to other Matters they Know nothing—the Germans deserting starving and useless, the French impudent and encroaching, and we pay heartily the poor Indians for this little quiet. yet at the beck of the French. they will molest us Again,[48] and it is not likely that they will be long quiet, I mean the Inhabitants. Green fits us with Solemnity & pace of Office and is the Knave and fool He Always Will be. However at the Head of the new england Party, for by the big Mans great good Menagement Open War is declared between them and the Old England people. I steer Clear of all these Affairs—thank God seldom spoke to, Not Even in the Affairs of my Own Office, for that of Register, the Secretary takes on Himself as Receiver—not a word said to Me except a Message by Cotterell to write to Gorham. I am easy tho' out of play—such connections are not desireable, and they All seem glad to leave me out. What they would be at, as Individuals, Is hard to guess. Perhaps they Know Not themselves.

From March the 1st to the third the coldest weather we have had this year and on the 1st this great affair of the Justices was finished in Open Court by a foolish speech compossed by Cotterell and spoke by Lawrence, Such As disobliged both the people and the Justices. Now I would have talked my own Nonsense or None had I been Lawrence, but this was a clear trick upon Him as supposed most in favor with the people. Yet Lawrence could not see it, and I shall not tell Him. the vanity of Mauger must now be apparent to Him. What

He means by all this disturbance He has given us Is onely to Bully Himself into the Council, and He would have succeeded did not I throw out a thwarting Oar. Any concessions is the Maxim, for peace sake, and that they Know and that makes them Insolent, I mean such as have money in their pockets, or say they have, and are supposed independant—but poor Rogues He crushes at Once and is inexorable. I stand as I did, counting the time when I shall see thee Dear Life. thank God I am in Health and Hope the Almighty will protect thee and My Little Girl.

to March 17th. the Weather has continued colder than the first part of the Winter, and much snow fell last night.

We are most truely in a State of Dullness and Inactivity, Not considering what is to be done with the Foreigners who are dying dayly thro' neglect, starved by that French Rascal Moreau who is to victual them. that fellow is much in favour, thro' Breynton who truely is the first Mover of Every thing. He has the Care of the Orphan House and sole disposer of All Our Charities—Great with all such as gave Mr Cornwallis trouble, consequently such Onely are prefered and Hearkened to. A Struggle between Breynton and that Fool Green and by playing of[f] the others at Green the Cause of All those Broils. Every Body in their turns swearing they will quit the Colony, but no fear of that while some get more Here than they can Elsewhere and Others Can Live No Where Else. to sum up the Whole He certainly pleases Nobody. Again such of the Foreigners as are Able are forming schemes to Desert to Lewisbourg, and I doubt not but we shall loose most part of them, for I can never think Zouberbulher Honest Who is to take Care of them.

March 17.

I am very well with the Colonel, but so Courtly that He is wonderous Fickle—but an Honest Man in the Main I think. Yet He is foolishly brought In to these parties. I Joyn Him as I care not what Commotions is Among them—Rogues All Which the Big Man could gaol had He the sense of a Goose or the Steddyness He Affects. For nothing can be more Ridiculous than bringing Poors Affair^{49} on the Carpet again to distress Green and Monk. tho' Rascals, it is Hard to look back into the first times of Mr Cornwallis for matter of impeachment Against them: and After He had reinstated Monk in His Commission. Who will serve such a Man when the Clamor of any Fool is sufficient Accusation and will be Heard with all solemnity under the pretend'd regard to Justice and disinterest[ed]ness? Yet with All these Formalities, anyone may see thro' the Big Man with half an Eye that those things are not so, are not as Pretended. I wish I may not be an unfortunate Instance of All this, For I intend next week to Ask leave to go Home in begining of April. To this He may demurr and If He does Demurr, it must be downright spite and Ill nature; for whatever use I might be of, He makes no use of me. As for His little slights of Me, and I despise the Man, I despise them Also.

My Dependance is On My Lord that this Man can not Essentially Hurt me; and please God Go I will whatever may be the consequence. For who in the situation, thank God, I am In and treated in the Manner I am would serve under such a Man? Yet notwithstanding Every ill treatment He may load me with, It shall never be said or suggested that my words or Actions could give Him Cause for it, Even to the most Minute Attention to My Duty, and the Respect Due to His Rank. Nor have I swerved a tittle from this point since I first served under Him. Yet thus it is with Me. the Honest Colonel will discourse much on this point, yet He can never make me beleive that the Moon is made of Green Cheese. Please God to Grant me Life and Health I shall once More Embrace my wife and Child, Whom God Preserve.

the Montbeliard People are dying for want of proper Care, and such of the Foreigners as are Able Depart. an outsettlement not fixed Yet. then such people are to be their rulers, as I dislike Zouberbula and Moreau, Who If faithfull in the Main to us will undoubt[ed]ly fleece them and force them to further desertion. So I have but a poor opinion of the outsettlement.

Saturday 24 March. 1753. Asked leave in the most Humble entreating manner, to return to England. refused it, under the most ridiculous Pretext, as the indispensable necessity of my continuing Here . . . Nobody more proper for the Employ &c. when not the least notice has been taken of me, but my employs encroached upon both as Rec^r and Reg^r. As makes it dishonourable for me in Person to Attend any longer. this refusal of His was therefore intended to make me outragious and depart without leave that He might have the filling up my Employments. the consideration onely of not satisfying those His Intentions makes me cringe, and use Every means to Obtain His Consent, for to give way to so apparent a scheme to distress my self would be the Highest imprudence, nor shall I either say or do any thing that may give Him even the shadow of offence. thus I Hope to disappoint His Soldier like Projects. God Bless my Poor Wife and Child—notwithstanding all this. Please God, we shall once more Embrace each other. The winter broke up and fine spring weather.

. . . Thursday April the 12th.⁵⁰ the Governor in Council told us that He intended the Casco Sloop to sail for England immediately. this was the first time I heard a word of this resolution and nothing can be more foolish considering the purpose She is Sent On—because the Lords of trade in a Letter arrived Here about the sixth Instant do not mention the provisions they are to send out. Now the Estimate for seventeen hundred is Allowed of by this Letter which gives the Credit at All Events [for] such provisions, and provision is at any time to be had not [i.e., on] the continent. but this they can not see, which if they did, there is no necessity for sending the Sloop to England, and they will be laughd at for their pains—but the point to be screened by this expedient Is their not sending the Foreign Settlers out and they are such bunglers we shall loose almost Every Man of them by Death and Desertion. And the Want of mentioning the word provision in the Letter from the Board of trade is the onely Excuse when Every body must see that the Allowing an Additional Number to be victualled in the last Estimate was giving them [the] desired credit, and consequently [the] Language of the Board of Trade. This was struck out by Lawrence and Cotterell while stood gapeing farcing very Clever. I am out of the Cabinet[51] but this is the reason given why I shall not have leave to return to England. I Know their intentions well enough Is to distress me so Here by neglect and such treatment, Yet to detain me under the pretence of the great use I am of—which they would have me really think neither—but so to detain me as to force me to throw up my Commission which He longs to dispose. All this History I have sent to Tom by Boston. My situation Here is most miserably, My poor wife and Child expecting me at Home As promised. Please we shall Once More meet again, and these people serve their private pique and their Friends by the spoils of my Commission. the last Letter from the Board has struck of[f] the Clerks in Office to fifty pounds a year and all the Overseers Engineers and such trash. Very properly for very extravagant sums were

"View of Halifax taken in July, 1757." Black and gray wash with black ink margins, by Benjamin Garrison. Courtesy Royal Ontario Museum.

given in all the offices—no less than a Hundred and sixty pounds yearly for Clerks onely besides Servants Attendants &c. It was onely Hard upon poor Collier but that I make up to His Old Salary, for my office was not of a farthing expence further than His Salary and Mine.

No Letters from My Lord Tom or the poor Hettys. surely they will take me out of this Bondage.[52] God Bless them all and Grant O God that we may Once more meet again.

This day I petitioned [the] Governor Most Humbly to return in the Casco, but from the Tenor of His behaviour read a Denial.[53] My reasons for going are unanswerable by Every One but an Absolute Prince determined to distress me, and this My Friend [Lawrence?] Joins In—Surely He is not absolutely let into the Big Mans Motives. I have more Charity for Him than to think so, and yet He must be blind not to see it. His prate and conciliating Nonsense is now become abominable and from this time forth shall think indifferently of Him. He has now fell in with Cotterell. tho' they hate one Another they Join to Jockey the Old Goose. A wise triumvirate and a Noble scheme sending this Sloop to England on such [35mm.].

Appendix A:
Letters

[*Salusbury to his wife, Hetty, Portsmouth–Plymouth, England, ?29 May 1749*]

My Dear Love. To live an individual—Not thought of by any body—Is of all Others, the Most Forelorne State: and, Except Thy Dear Self, Life, I am the Very Man.

I think, perhaps, I could have laid Aside My Own Honour, Ambition, call it what you will, For the Happyness, the Joy of being always with thee: But then, not to be Able to Live up to Thy Rank, without this Prostitution of That Joy, Determined Me. This then, is onely to be considered, that in the light I am now In, Nothing, I fear, can be saved from my Income So as to support our Happyness hereafter. That I should Devour All without Thee A Partaker is not the thing I mean—quite the Reverse. Why then All this Prostitution of Our Onely Joy at Our Age?

I Know what others Mean—Nothing but to be thrown Out of the Way; Being out of sight Answers the End of Some—with the truely Honble Addition of Drinking that Health they Assist not to Support, therefore Urge On to the means of it's Destruction.

Notwithstanding this, I am Wonderfully well, Thank God; Conscious I can do my Duty, Even anything another Can—or Dare. Let then Governors, Colonels or Captains be wise or Foolish as they please—It affects not Me. Nothing, Upon My Soul, Can but this Separation from Thee, not all the confinement at Sea with it's Nastyness and Ribaldry—could a Voyage be Supposed without any Real Hazard. God Bless thee My Dear Life, take Care of thy Self and the poor little Girl If it was for My sake onely. My Onely Hope My Onely Comfort— —that we may be Once More Happy—Truely never to part again: And I Trust in the Almighty it shall Be So Amen.

Hold up thy Heart Dear Love. Please God we shall meet Again: What greatly assists to Support Mine Is that I am out of the reach of their Snears or Insults and Fairly Practice Every Honest Endeavour to gain an Independancy. the twenty Nin'th of May, no Happy Day to me—nor Any other, Absent from My Dear Love—Is the day I got Here and write this from Portsmouth. we sailed on Monday last as I told you.[1] I expected a Letter Here, disappointments fret me. why had not you wrote? Grant O God You are All Well. I shall write next post. today is Friday. Plymouth. Yours Most Affectionatly, J. Salusbury.

[Salusbury to Hetty, Halifax, N.S., 19 August? 1749]

. . . If it was altogether Indian it would be uncommon and diverting: but we are an English Colony, and figure to your self the Tower, Billingsgate and Wapping—you have it. In time it is to be Hop'd we shall get a little further into the Country, have roads &c and then a snug farm will be comfortable enough, for the Climate is certainly Healthy and not too warm, tho' some complain. the Account they give of the Clear frosts in winter can not be disagreeable. We are wood'd Everywhere with timber of all sorts to the very waters Edge and as impassable as the strongest thicket in Bachagraig woods; and this all the Country Over except a little at Minas and Annapolis. the French, poor wretches, tho' numerous, very little different in Colour or superior in understanding to the Indians themselves. the Bason and Harbor of Chibouctou very fine, Answers exactly to the Chart of it, with plenty of fish.

the town of Halifax is in all the forwardness that can be expected in the time; all Hands employ'd in the Publick work to get under shelter before winter: so that the lots of land are not as yet given Out and that part of my Employ not come On. Coll. Gorham who Commands the Indian Rangers in Our Service Is soon to go to Minas and so on to Annapolis by land, and If I can Obtain leave will take the Jaunt with Him.

I am with the Governor on board the beaufort, as there is no place as yet to Shelter us Ashore—All the Inhabitants live in tents on the Ground they have clear'd. I wish I had the Dogs tom promis'd me for I am grown quite dumb, converse with nobody except the Indian Coll[onel] when I get at Him, and the Dogs would be excellent Company for us both in Our Journey—when I return I shall have news to tell you.

[*Salusbury to Hetty, Halifax, N.S., 16 July 1750*]
My Dear Life.

My Heart akes when I write to thee—when and where will this Letter find thee—God Knows. Please God we shall once more meet, never to part again. I have the strongest Hopes I shall be in England about the latter end of the Year, and in the way agreeable to Us both, and without that I will not stir from Hence. Being sent to England on the Province affairs will be a great Honor done Me: and I am sure any thing of that kind will be approved of by my Honble Patron Lord Halifax and very much Esteemed Friend Dr Crane: but should their sentiments differ in this point, for some particular reasons I Know not: I shall ever be all Obedience to their Commands. I long for the Arrival of the shiping from England, for I doubt not having Letters that will satisfy me in this Affair of the utmost importance, Dear Love, to our Happyness: and till then, I am now so much in the dark, I can say nothing, with Certainty, on that Head further than, had I my Choice, I had much rather embrace thee and my little Girl in England. therefore, if you find it not disagreeable to His Lordship and Crane, press it as far as is proper. I have said all I could on this subject in my Letter to Dr Crane by this Ship. Please God we shall meet again. I have my Health wonderfully well—no fatigue Hurts me thank God—tho' the weather is now very Hot, and in my travells I never get on Horseback.

I recd Your fine coat, it is much too fine, as I grudge the Price: tho' people dress Here, which is Strange, extravagantly.I constantly Attend Our Court but had rather be with thee in a Cottage than at the Head of All our American Affairs without thee; I want thee Dear Love for My Friend, My Assistant.

I recd Every thing You and Tom sent me by Maugers and

the Roehampton and to be thus taken Notice of gave me much reputation &c &c. tell Tom I will write to Him if the ship sails not directly, but I could not bundle another Letter into My Lords Packet, and His I will not fail to get ready at all Events.

God almighty bless thee My Dear Love and poor little Hetty.

> Thine Most Affectionatly
> J. Salusbury.

Halifax Nova Scotia Monday 16th July 1750.

[Salusbury to Hetty, Halifax, N.S., 17 July 1750]
My Dear Love.

I inclose this in a Letter to Sir Lynch, but I say nothing to Him of my Hopes of being in England before winter, and on the footing You approve of. Lord Halifax will send You a Letter from me, for I have also inclosed one in His packet: and very glad I am that I have finished every thing I have to say to His Lordship and Crane, for I am order'd to be ready tomorrow Morning to go on board Rous to reconnoître the Coast westward of our Port. we have a very strong party, and if the Governor can spare time, goes Himself[2]—and this ship may possibly sail before our return.

As she is bound to Liverpool (Called the Sarah) I send Sir Lynch some of our fish, the fellow I employ'd to cure me Cods tongues and Zounds[3] is not returned from the fishing banks, Furs are not to be had. these cursed Indians plague Us So—worked up and Assisted by the French to do it, but thank God they can not Hurt us much.

I wish I could do poor ned Price any Service, to no Man living am I better Inclined, and will try every thing in my power should He come, but I fear Our Winter would be too severe for His Husky constitution.

Tom has done very well in sending me the dogs and every thing—something, any thing from England gives great reputation Here. the Cheese and Drinkables I gave the Governor as I am always at His table—one of the Family. God bless thee Dear Life and Grant thee Health and Peace of Mind and that we may once More embrace each other. God bless poor little Hetty.

Thine Most Affectionatly
J. Salusbury.

I am not obliged to go on these expeditions, but the Governor approves of it and trusts particularly to the Accounts I give Him. Hans Fowler[4] has not appeared Here Yet. I must write to Tom and then I have done, it is now very late.

Halifax Nova Scotia tuesday July 17th 1750.

the great increase of this settlement is truely wonderfull. It is rather a party of pleasure that we go on tomorrow than any thing else, but there is no stiring there without Arms and in a Warlike Manner.

Say something from Me to Honest Dick Lloyd.[5] I would have wrote to Him by this ship but for these orders.

I hint my coming to Tom—if not disagreable to His Lordship—and to try that point. It would be much to my Honor did the Orders come from My Lord—but if He likes it not—Not a Word More.

[*Salusbury to Hetty, Halifax, N.S., 20 September 1750*]

Dear Life. I thought when I wrote last that I might have depended on an Honble Message to England the later end of this year, but see it now impracticable, and without some such permission Dear Love should have feared that even You Yourself, as much as we long to be together, would not in Judgement have approved it; besides to have deserted the Governor and leave Him quite Alone would not perhaps be well thought of at Bashy.[6] All this Dear Love is too great a self Denial and Mortif[ic]ation—and truely to me paying too dear for my Employment. Had I thought this I think now that I would have beg'd of you to come Here, tho' the thoughts of such a voyage without me is what I can not bear to think of—Nor shall not be. Mr Davidson the Secretary returns with this ship to answer divers Impeachments &c &c.

Now the fellow is tumbling All our people Cry out against Him. that He is a Scotch pedlar I always perceived, and told it Crane fairly. I am one of the Comittee Here to inspect His accompts and have sat six hours those three last days, Every day six Hours on that bussiness, and You Know How I love Accoumpts. He is such a fellow as Paynter, French onely excepted, but in Accompts not so Clever. After breaking up at the Governors table at Eleven I began this Letter. we sit again at these same Accompts tomorrow at nine in the Morning and when that is Over the America sails with this and them the first fair wind—

So I will sit with thee Dear Love as long as my eyes are open. Oh How I wish we could close them together. All this to live thus seperated Is too much—for what—for Money. I have now declined their money employment—Knowing I will be Honest *think* it too much trouble: on that footing not worth while to have Governments Money in Keeping. My Sole Aim is being agreeable to the Governor and well with all Honest Men. this winters confinement Here, which I reckon'd to be released from, vex's my very soul. God Help thee and poor little Hetty. Keep up thy spirits Dear Love for in April next or before I shall sail for England. I had like to have said I will. for this purpose I sollicited My Lord Himself in my last. I could Hold out no longer. I wish He may not be displeased at it: but I put it thus Not out of any dislike to my situation, but to return with thee and the little wench. In this manner You must second my sollicitation at Every opportunity &c. I am so distracted in my self without thee (I let nobody see it) that nothing pleases me but Drums Marching &c. I had been gone with Lawrence had I not Hopes of seeing thee this winter. March I can with any of 'em or do any thing where the Head is not much concern'd. I love Lawrence and All our Soldier lads Love Me. I do not grudge them their Honours in this last Action, but I had a Kind of right to partake, as I stood Stoutly runing away last time—and it is well we did, or we had been scalp'd to [a] Man.

Honest Lawrence deserves well for the fatigues He undergoes. Our new Regiment[7] is startled devilishly at the

Service. Our Ragamuffins (had we had Numbers sufficient) would have done as well—a forced retreat in any Country, especialy in this, is a much more dismaying circumstance than a brisk action with any tolerable success, but this last was very well and doubt not but it will answer the good End intended, the security of the Province. I do not mean our settlement Here but the Whole Peninsula.

Poor Cousin Hans is come, and the first time I saw him He was something like sober—Never have seen Him any thing like sober since—and what is worse came into the Governors swagering as if at Salop,[8] till the Guards turn'd Him out, and finding that noise will not do, gives Us Here less trouble now, but has been often in the Constables hands. Good night. this foolish fellow sets me asleep. I wish I may dream of thee. I never did Here but once and that is very strange. It is very Cold to night the Wind NW—the day was remarkably warm.

God bless thee and the poor little Hetty is all I can say to thee this day six oclock Evening. I must now close my Letter.
Thine and Thine onely Most Affectionatly
                              J. Salusbury.

Halifax Sepr 20th 1750.

I have wrote to thee by every ship all this summer from Annapolis &c—pray write and send it by way of Boston to Hancock.[9] I Love nothing but reading thy Letters. I have 'em all by me.

Speak to Crane if You can. I write to Him by this ship.

[*Salusbury to Hetty, Halifax, N.S., 5 February? 1751*]
My Dear Hetty.

God Almighty Bless and Protect thee and the poor little Girl. You see I can not slip any opportunity of writing to thee, but am very uneasy that I do not Hear from thee—the last dated at Combermere came by a Liverpool ship: Yet I am in Hopes that You have wrote by way of Boston and that I shall receive them in time. It is now febry 5th thank God—Yet time laggs too much for my Impatience to Embrace thee and the little Girl—Never More, Please God, to Part again—thine Most Affectionatly.

J. Salusbury.

Halifax, Nova Scotia.

[*Salusbury to Hetty, Halifax, N.S., 28 June 1751*]
My Dear Life.

Nothing but the Hopes of seeing thee soon could keep me in my Senses these several put off's so distract me. the vessel that brings this I most certainly thought to have sailed In.

Being Under the command of another, especially in my present circumstances, is the very Devil: However I behave so as to give no Offence—but God onely Knows How it Hurts me to be thus detained. there is a Vessel now building Here to sail very soon; In her I am determined, as much determined as my situation will Allow Me, at All Events to Sail—and Please God we may once more meet again. God Almighty Bless thee and my poor little Girl and Grant that we may soon Embrace each other.

I am so distressed between Hope and fear that I can write no More. please God we shall soon talk all those distress's over.

Thine Most Affectionatly
J. Salusbury.

Halifax Nova Scotia June 28th 1751.

[*Salusbury to Hetty, Plymouth, England, 6 June 1752*]
Friday I wrote to thee My Dear Life. this is saturday Morning June 6th going on board and sail directly. In the situation I am Now In—since it must be so—the onely thing that Hurts Me Is that I have not recd a Letter from thee since I have been Here now upwards of a week—and I have wrote Every post. this gives me cruel apprehensions for thee and the poor little Girl Least All should not be well with You. God Almighty forbid that any Harm should come to thee My Onely Joy, my Onely Comfort. God Almighty Bless and Protect You Both and Grant that we may be Once More Happy together Amen. Thine Most Affectionatly. J. Salusbury.

[*Salusbury to Hetty, Funchal, Madeira, 28 June 1752*]
My Dear Dear Life.

I have ten thousand Hopes and Fears about thee. Receiving no Letters at Plymouth makes me fear some mishap to thee or my poor little Girl I was not to Hear of: This I strongly fear and am cruel uneasy. Then again I Hope, Yet can Hope but faintly, that All is well with you Both, that You went to the old Lady's[10]—or somewhere out of the reach of my Letters, and that some fool perswaded thee that we should sail from thence before thy Letters could get there.

we had a fortnights and three days passage to Madeira. nothing uncommon, but the usual sea way: Ribaldry, Nonsense and Nastyness enough to confound or Poyson any Mortal, except fish of their Own Element. I am sure that the disagreeableness, as aforesaid, of a Voyage, exclusive of Every thing else, exclusive of my Absence from Thee, Is a Sufficient Sacrafice to any Friendship, and the Honor accrueing from such a Service purchased at full Value. I say it is onely Honor—the substantials would make me much More satisfied with myself.

This Island is the exact Look of our Country about Traêth Mawr,[11] a body of Entire Hills and Rocks with the like Breaks in them. the difference Is, that every Interval of soil is planted with the Vine, so far up the Hills to the place where the Clouds descend, and this constantly is the Case, in Summer, from about ten in the Morning till night; so it is from sunrise onely till that Hour you can see the Summit (and a Noble Prospect it is). this then preserves a Verdure and gives a Coolness to the Air which would otherwise, most certainly, be much too Hot.

The Inhabitants (and they are very Numerous) might be rich from their wine trade, but that they are Charged with such multitudes in the Priesthood; and being Portuguese Inherit their National Pride, Laziness and Nastyness. Even In the English Houses their Furniture and Flooring is much of a Peice with Our Inn at Tanŷbulch.[12] their Fruits are mean because not cultivated; Cherrys, Pears, Apricocks, Peaches. I have eat much better in England. Their figs pretty good, tho' they tell me the best sort is not ripe Yet. they make a Sweetmeat of their Citron which I have not tasted but will order some to Tom. I send two pipes of Wine to Him. if that be too much, My Lord or Sir Lynch will be glad of One. the foolish Flowers made by their Nuns—the worst I ever saw either as to Fancy or Execution.

It was ridiculous not to have some Credentials to this place, for a Merchant might take me for an Imposter—Not that I want any thing on My Own Account, but to be at Madeira and not send a pipe or two of Wine to England is a thing never done. when this same Wine will come I can not guess at. it must be ship't to the West Indies first and so Home, for not twice a year do Ships go from Hence immediatly to England.

I am promised that this Letter shall go by way of Lisbon, tho' the Wines must not, because of Duty &c &—thank God I have my Health very Well Even in this very Hot place. I hope to stand the freezing at Nova Scotia as well as I do frying Here. God Almighty Bless and Protect thee My Dear Life and My poor little Girl; and Grant O God that we may Once More Meet Again and I promise thee never to undertake again these expeditions of Honor.

> Thine Most Affectionatly.
> J. Salusbury.

about this time next year please God I will be at Home. If I receive not a Letter from thee at Halifax I shall run almost Mad. God Bless thee My Dear Love.

> Funshal In Madeira.
> June 28th 1752.

[*Salusbury to Hetty, Halifax, N.S., 12 August 1752*]
My Dear Life. thank God that thou art Well. I have recd two scolding Letters from thee in return to my Numbers. I do not care How much you scold so that You are but Both Well. Our scolding is not onely of equal insignificancy to each of Us, but proceeds from much the same cause.

I wrote to thee from Madeira. Nothing to be sent from thence but Wine. the season for Citron not begun, but the Merchant promised to send some directed to Tom, When ready. I bought for Tom two pipes of Wine and drew a bill on Him for the payment.

God Bless thee. take Care of thy self and the poor little Girl. I can never be easy seperated thus. It must not be thus Long—It shall not please God— and please God we meet again—never will part again. Thy Letter by way of Boston I have not recd, and this is the first I write to thee from Hence by way of New York.

Governor Cornwallis wonderfull Civil &c to Me now. Mr Hopson in point of experience will never be rude, tho' formality and Distance &c &c be of the very essence of Government. Lawrence the same Man I left Him. that I did not write to thee sooner—I was taken up with a long Letter of Politics &c to the Peer (which I sent by way of Boston). in great Hopes of Peace with the Indians but now we have no Chance I think, for they have begun Hostilities again; and have taken some of our people not indeed immediatly at our door, but on the fisheries to the Eastward. but not a Word of this, except you think it proper to my Friend Crane. I must tell thee further that Our treasury Here is so poor that it would be almost a shame to draw on it, so I must draw on tom at Home, and remit my bills to You on Kilby to repay Him. about twenty pound present was thought right I should give my Mess on board the Jason. So You find it impossible to travel for nothing either by sea or Land, and much vexed I am to be thus squandring, by my self, what would make us Happy together—Nor can a World—If that World thou Did'st not partake of—Give me a Moments satisfaction.

Not one of them will think of me if thou does not remind them. any thing in Ireland—there we may be together—and still more pleasant as out of their way—and that may be no small motive with them neither—therefore think of Ireland.

Depend upon it, I will not outstay my time Here—if I can Hold it that long—yet never fear my doing any thing Over rash or Imprudent.

God Almighty Bless thee my Dear Love and Poor little Girl—bid Her continue Her Journal.

I shall relapse again if any ship arrives without a Letter. I have no time to write to Tom but tell Him of this Money Matter.

Thine most Affectionatly.

J. Salusbury.

August 12th 1752 Halifax Nova Scotia.

[*Salusbury to Hetty, Halifax, N.S., 16 October 1752*]
My Dear Life.

I have nothing to say. I truely can say nothing; Nor is any thing worth the saying except Best Wishes—Blessings—and my Prayers that All Health and Happyness may be thy Lot and my poor little Girls. This (as all my Letters) come inclosed to Tom. This by the Hound Sloop of War Capⁿ Dove, In which ship I send six Quintal of fish, and Eleven Caggs[13] of Zounds. My Lord Halifax to Have what He Likes, the rest as You and Tom may agree. there are also a Few skins directed to Tom, but those are All thy Own to do as You please with.

I have nothing else to send thee my Dear Love, except the Inclosed Bill, of which forty pounds is already Due to Tom by my Draught on Him payable to Mr Baker some time since. the three Hundred pound Bill you must pay Mr Kilby with, and take His receipt. You Know I am but a bad menager —besides that I have been Cheated, downright Cheated of forty pounds; it is true. I saw it, but could not Help my self, it vexed me Indeed—but the story is too long to tell thee Now.

So that for the time to come, I shall draw on Tom for what I shall expend Here, but will take Care that my Salary shall always be sufficient to Answer it. Never will have any thing more to do with the Paltry Rascalls Here: and Please God, Dear Love, will endeavour to get from Hence before next May is Over; and if no Vessels offer Here, will work my passage either by Boston or New York, Once More to Embrace thee and the poor little Girl Never to part again—Truely Never. Thy Letters by way of Boston must have all miscarry'd for I have recd None.

Dear Love I can write no More. Here is nothing but Dullness, the very Empire of Dullness. If I have not a Letter from thee soon and a Journal from poor Hetty I shall be very unhappy. Hetty must not expect Letters from me—tell Her.

My Dear Love God Almighty Bless thee and the poor little Girl. Thine Most Affectionatly. J. Salusbury.

Mr Cornwallis has been excessive Civil to Me since I came last. Lawrence always the Same.

Staying Here six Months Longer I think is the Highest Compliment I could pay His Lordship, whatever He may think of it. I am sure I would not have done it but to Endeavour to please—and that it was His pleasure it should be So.

Halifax Oct 16th 1752.

Frank[14] I fear will turn out a Rascal—I could have bore with His Drunkeness tolerably.

[*Salusbury to Hetty, Halifax, N.S., 10 December 1752*]

My Dear Life. I Know not How it is, tho' I think of nothing Else but thee, Yet I can not write to thee as I write to other Folk. I am wonderfully well thank God. that thou and my poor little Girl may be also in Health, and that we may continue So—Once More to Embrace Each other—is the Sum the Whole Sum of my Hopes and wishes; except further —that the Almighty may so Protect Us that no consideration on Earth may cause another separation.

I have wrote a long Narrative to My Lord and Tom —perhaps you may Hear nothing of it, but in Enigmatick Questions. the substance of it Is that Our King Logg with a double G attempts dayly encroachments on my Employs; And I cry out Lustily for Help. Let His Lordship support those Employs, I will not stand Battleing it Here, and be money out of Pocket. Here then Is my Vexation, I shall not come Home worth a Groat; and I am sure I deserve Money, for Live Here.

You may expect me Home some time next summer, but when Is not in my Power to say, nor ought You to think. this

Money Affair, not to be able to save a farthing, grieves me beyond expression; and yet I live as spareingly as I Can. I have not sixpence advantage. My bare Salary Onely—and that with my poor menagement, will bring In Nothing at the Years End. but this I will take care of—Not to Exceed My Income—And to Mend this matter. that Rascal Frank has played the Devil. Drunk, eternally Drunk since He first smelt tar with me, Lost and Embezled almost Every thing He had of Mine. Says that You gave Him no Inventory of what He had under his Care. I can find none among my papers, so that in that respect must take what He gives Me. and to complete the fullness of His Idleness, One Night, in the Lone House I have taken, where onely He and I lived together, What did the Rascal attempt but to beat me as I was stripped going to bed. However In this I gave Him his Deserts, Kicked Him out of Doors—Scarce Able to crawl to a Lodgings. Yet I Have paid this Rascal Every farthing He demanded, gave Him every thing He made any pretence to, never punished Him in the Law way, as I might have done very severely; and before this particular insolence on His part never gave Him an Angry Word; but bore with His Drunkkeness and Neglects with all forbearance. Rot Him, I will say No More of the Rascal.

Yet it vexed me more than all the Attempts of King Log in power to distress me, if you will except money matters onely. Log I totally despise—can do my Duty—therefore a fart for Him.

I am in such Health, thank God, take so much care of my self, that I sink under nothing in point of Spirit, this money matter once more excepted. Let me beg of thee Dear Hetty to keep up thy Old Heart.

Besides Dear Love this is the Tenth day of December, according to the regulation, and I shall make what Haste I can to thaw in thy Arms. God Almighty Bless thee My poor Dear Love and My poor little Girl.

Thine Most Affectionatly. J. Salusbury. We are not fit to live apart.

It is deadly cold, and wood as Dear as at Dunstable:[15] and I am in the same poor naked House with my New Man, who formerly lived with Lady Charlotte's Major Johnston.[16] His Name Is Lowe, and left His Service on an unfortunate affair Tom will tell you of. He behaves very well as Yet, and Hope he will continue so.

If you see Crane tell Him I have always wrote a scrap to Him in Every Packet except this; but have not recd a Line from either My Lord or Him since I came Here, and but One Letter from Tom. Yours My Dear and poor Hetty's Journals I have had till about the 3^d of August.

God Bless thee My Dear Hetty and my poor little Girl—please God We Shall Once More meet again Never More to part.

[*Salusbury to Hetty, Halifax, N.S., ?March 1753*]
My Dear Love. God bless thee and thanks for all thy Letters. I beleive most of them are now come tho' I did not receive them till the 8th of febry last. You know I never had the best patience, but America will teach me. I have not yet recd your present of the warming pan, the Gun, or poor little Hetty's tokens. God bless the poor little Girl. I Hope she continues very Good as I left Her.

God Knows what the Event[17] is of the last proposal I sent you, to consult Dr Crane upon. Shall we meet again or How My Dear Love? I can neither determine nor think of any thing till I Know the Event of that. the Letter that brought this proposal was sent to Tom by one Mr Major.[18] this only I am determined upon, that I will not quit my employ as long as Lord Halifax is at the Head of the board[19] but according to my proposal I Might enjoy it, and come to England at least to fetch you over, for if I am doom'd to Live Here, I will not Live without thee, if thou can'st think of residing in the wilderness. this last winter would have been terrible to thee to the last degree. dayly Alarms of the Enemy attacking Us—All the Inhabitants constantly under Arms: we can not get at them to come to Action, and without destroying them we can Hope for No peace.

Our great Case is to prevent the Enemy from surprising us.

that is their manner of fighting and they are expert Enough at it. It is the cursed popish priests that encourage those poor wretches. they might else live happy enough with us and be of use in fishing and bringing Game, furs &c. as they were at first. and great fools they were, since they have begun, not begin at first; then they might have gone near routing us or confin'd us to One of the little Islands in [the] Mouth of the Harbor in the Dead of Winter. when we had more than three foot snow on the Ground the weather very Cold, were these wretches assembling from vast Distances to Attack Us. In Our turn now we are sending Arm'd Sloops and marching Cross the Count[r]y to seek for them. to find them is the difficulty. when found they are easyly got the better of. being thus employ'd we had little or no fur this Winter, and what the neutral french brought was so bad and so very Dear that a Gentleman Here who understands furs told me, Much better might be had in London and for less Money—so I send none to you or Sir Lynch who I think would like something of that Kind. A Gentleman made me a present of an Indian Purse and I send it little Hetty to give Lady Halifax or Her little Ones should they fancy it—but this as you please—if you like it Highly Keep it Your Self.

I recd two Letters from Lord Halifax and one from Crane all extremely Kind. His Lordship is pleased to say things that I don't deserve. Pinfold[20] has been so Good as to write Me. you must thank Pinfold. I have not time—besides I am dab at writing.

Tom in His Old Style gave me the History of Sir Lynch's Election I suppose but truely without straining the Matter. I could only suppose it; for to this Hour I can not make it out farther than that He was a Mighty Actor in the Affair.[21] In that Tom pleased me, if He was any way instrumental in bringing it to bear: Not out of any peevishness I bear My [30 mm.] Wynne[22] and their foolish Clan; but that I wish Sir Lynch Every Honor His Rank and fortune entitle Him to. if He likes not a Gallop, His Prudence will not trust so far to old Time, as not to Keep on a travelling pace now He is in the

Great road. I think you could set Him as right as any body, because I Know You love Him better.

God Help, bless and protect thee, And the little wench, Dear Love. I want thee dayly to talk what should be right, and to Determine What is. Nothing Here is so banefull to me as the want of such a Friend as thou Art. thank God I am now well in Health—and well respected— but I fought it up Hill and without a Friend to Assist Me, till Lord Halifaxs last Letters Feb^{ry} 8th last recd Here—and they closed up the whole. I am at a Loss to Know who could give the Governor a bad impression of Me, except Bodville[23] or Lord Herbert,[24] Moved thereunto by a Spirit the reverse of Right, because I had in a very particular Manner served them; and for this reason I particularly suspect and point at them.

I have twenty shilling a Day and for that, do my Duty in my Station, with a regularity not to be gain say'd, and the subordination that becomes Me. Upon this Plan I proceeded and Every thing does well. My Dear Hetty I am speaking to You. therefore not a word of this to Tom Crane or Any body. I like twenty shilling a Day and for less will never come into England but on the proposal I made in my last. Grant O God it may succeed.

Now we have a little respite from the Enemy I most heartily wish thee Here, unhappy thou art not Here for ten thousand reasons, but then when the great Clamour comes I rejoyce thou art any where else. I spend too [much] money, My Love, but I then Keep up my Rank, and truely squander not sixpence but with that view: whether that is right or No I am much in doubt— — it is altogether experimental—but Observe this, that I am greatly within the bounds of my Income and Hope to send thee some little money at the Years end, tho' I am building a fishing Schooner which will take near a Hundred pounds. I Knew it would please my Lord, So have flourish'd it out to Him.[25] My Dear Life take Care of thy self. have every thing that is proper. Creditors I never contracted with, or contracted with to save others should stay. You have the best right and use it My Dear. God Bless thee—take Care of thy self—and Know that I would not give a Rash to Live but in Hopes One Day Once More to Embrace thee Dear Love and My poor little Girl. for that reason I am Stout and nothing shall Hurt Me please God; and I think strongly we shall once More Embrace NEVER to part again. but How to fix this and when the *Long When* will come, depends on Your Answer to my Proposals by Major. Sir Lynch tho' a Good Man is to[o] contracted for Me to Hope for any employment in England thro' His influence; not but He certainly might do it: but as Affairs now stand I think it not prudent to Grasp at a Shadow and was it equally convenient to you Could with pleasure finish an Indian Campain—half a dozen of 'em at Least. Thank God I am in Good Health and have been so except about three weeks, vex'd a little too much and had the Jaundice. the Account we had of Lord Halifax's ill Health topp'd it, and during that time I had strange Whims; thought You all Dead, and my self deserted &c yet strong as these whims were I had not a friend to trust with the secret, to give me the least Comfort: but all the letters came febry the 8th. I rejoyc'd and was soon well. I wonder How Crane could tell you I liv'd at Colliers, I have liv'd all the While at the Governors, and had passive stoutness to stand it all, and behaved so that no body could see I was out of Humour or perceive what I so plainly saw—or thought I saw. the Governor is truely a Good Honest Man. His Character in this light and Every other is very Justly His Due. If I am not a particular favourite of His, I am so with everyone in the Colony—His Secretary excepted, and I suspect a little Jealousy for that. You Know my Vanity, and it is fairly pardonable, if to be well with ones Contemporaries and on a Just footing, can be called such. Why is Sophy and [Lioney?] so queer? the Old Lady I Heartily wish well and the Good widow. To Sir Lynch and His family Every Respects with ten thousands thanks. Dear Love, God bless thee and little Hetty, thine Most Affectionatly

J. Salusbury.

I expect in April a Letter from thee that will determine[26] my fears and give me Joy, I hope.

[*Salusbury to Governor Hopson? Halifax, N.S., April 1753*]

. . .But In the Case of Mr Poor, a Settler, at that time, of as much Property as Most Among Us, Risqued also on the Wellfare of the Colony—I say that in this Case to suppose Piracy from such a Man Must be Wholely Affected—Mere Pretext—Ridiculous—If not Worse, tending to Views I am ashamed to Hint at.

The Fact, Sir, the truth of the Fact is this—two small Coasters fell into One of Our Harbors to the Eastward. Mr Poor was In One of them from Newfoundland—the other from Lewisbourg as they Know by the Course. Poors people Haled them and wanted some of their Rum or Brandys. the Others, conscious they were on a Contraband Trade, slipt their Cabel and made to see [sea], Not fearing Poors people as Pyrates, But in Doubt whether they did not belong to His Majesty to Intercept that scandalous Trade so successfully Carried On between the Colonies and Lewisbourg.

I shall make no further Observations But submit the rectitude of such measures to Your Excellencys consideration.

this is the truth of the Fact, this the mighty All that was to have brought Mr Poor to the Gallows. Here they failed, but that this prosecution in part Ruined Mr Poor Is Certain: and thus far they succeeded I Know nothing but Hearsay &c.

But at the time Mr Poor was prosecuted for Piracy, I had the Honor of a seat at this Honble Board: And full well remember the Prosecution to be most solemnly Introduced, and Most learnedly Exaggerated to a Degree scarce heard Of, Even to the Imprisoning of Mr Poors Person, without Bail or Mainprise. I could not Assent to this Proposal without remonstrating that In so doing the Laws must be Highly strained.

I therefore made it appear to Mr Cornwallis that the Crime of Piracy was bailable at this Board, and Mr Poor was Bailed According (this Mr Collier Knows).

Little did I Guess at the Point Aimed At, Else Far be it from me to Disconcert the Measures of any Great Man. For you must Know, Sir, that Had Mr Poor been Immediatly

Clapt in Prison, so unfortunate a Situation Must Have greatly Quickened a Bargain then Negotiating between Mr Monk
and Mr Poors Wife;[27] and pressed on the Part of Mr Monk
with much Retorick, expressing Much Kindness Also to the
poor Woman in Distress, and this Bargain was of no less consequence Sir than the Utter Ruin of Mr Poor His Wife and
Children in Stripping them of All they had in the World.

Actual and Real Piracy, On the neighbouring Seas, Is One
of the Worst Evils that can Happen to an Infant fishing Colony. And to prevent such If possible—Or to Deter men from
it No Precaution—No punishment too Great. But in the
Case, Actual and real Pyracy on the neighbouring seas, Is one
of the Greatest Evils that can befall an Infant fishing Colony;
therefore to prevent such, Every Precaution necessary
—Every punishment Lawfull.

Appendix B:
Biographical Sketches

The individuals sketched below are related in some significant way to the life of John Salusbury or connected with the
establishment of Halifax but not adequately discussed in the
journal. Others who might belong here are already accounted
for in the introduction or footnotes and may therefore be
located in the index. Taken together, these individuals are a
cross-section of the soldiers and civilians engaged in settling
the colony or influencing it more remotely in English social or
official circles. A variety of manuscript and printed sources
yielded the information. Particularly useful were the *Dictionary of Canadian Biography* (Toronto: University of
Toronto Press), vols. 3 (1974) and 4 (1979), and C. B.
Fergusson's *Directory of the Members of the Legislative
Assembly of Nova Scotia, 1759–1958* (Halifax: Public Archives of Nova Scotia, 1958).

ANWYL, REVEREND WILLIAM. Anwyl had served as a
naval chaplain before accompanying Cornwallis to Nova
Scotia as a missionary of the Society for the Propagation of the
Gospel, but the Welsh priest soon exhibited some of the worst
habits of the naval service. In December 1749, his superior,
Tutty, reported to the S.P.G. that "his whole Conduct and
Conversation, both his Actions and Expressions Bespeak
rather the Boatswain of a Man of War than the Minister of the
Gospel of Christ." Although Anwyl was severely reprimanded
by the governor, his continued excessive drinking rendered
him incapable of carrying out any priestly functions. Finally,

his salary was suspended and Moreau was appointed in his place; but before he could be sent home, Anwyl died in February 1750. When his register could not be found, the governor issued a proclamation causing all those Anwyl had married to declare themselves to Tutty.

BARTELO, CAPTAIN FRANCIS. Cornwallis rated this officer higher than John Gorham in the campaign against the Indians in 1749–50. In February 1750, he successfully led a party of troops to apprehend Girard, the Cobequid priest, as well as the deputy at Cobequid who had stopped a Halifax courier and otherwise aided the Indians. In April, he was appointed commander of all independent companies in the province and served as second in command to Lawrence during the Chignecto expedition that month. He was killed in a skirmish during the second expedition to Chignecto in September.

BASTIDE, JOHN HENRY. Bastide became the most influential military engineer in Nova Scotia when he was appointed chief engineer of Annapolis Royal in 1740. For the next two decades he was a prominent figure in both Nova Scotia and New England and took part in both sieges of Louisbourg. In 1757, when engineers were first granted a military rank, he was promoted to lieutenant-colonel and became a lieutenant-general in 1770.

BREWSE, JOHN. Brewse came to Halifax with Cornwallis as the latter's engineer and as such drew up the first plan for the town. He was also appointed one of the first justices of the peace. Wounded during the second expedition to Chignecto in 1750, he later served at Louisbourg after its capture in 1758 and elsewhere and was a lieutenant-colonel when he died in 1781.

BREYNTON, REVEREND JOHN. John Breynton was born in Wales in 1719. After graduating from Cambridge University, he was ordained in 1742 and became a chaplain in the Royal Navy. After serving in a series of sea appointments, he accompanied a squadron to Louisbourg in 1746 and served as deputy chaplain until the evacuation of 1749. Returning to England, he became a missionary of the Society for the Propagation of the Gospel and was sent to Halifax in 1752 to relieve William Tutty, who had been granted permission to return to England to marry. With the death of Tutty, Breynton shared the pastoral duties of Saint Paul's Church with another missionary, the Reverend Thomas Wood. Salusbury saw him, in the role of dispenser of public charities, as a meddler in government affairs. Appointed rector of Saint Paul's in 1759, he remained in Halifax until 1789 and died in England in 1799.

BULKELEY, RICHARD. Bulkeley was perhaps the most outstanding of all the settlers who arrived with Cornwallis. Born in Ireland, he was a dragoons officer when he was appointed Cornwallis's aide-de-camp in 1749. He was editor of the *Halifax Gazette*, Canada's first newspaper, when it started in 1752, and subsequently became a judge of the Vice Admiralty Court, the first churchwarden of Saint Paul's Church, a grand master of the freemasons, and a brigadier-general of militia. In 1759, he was appointed a member of council and secretary of the province and held this position until 1793. His first wife was the daughter of Captain John Rous (q.v.).

DU CHAMBON, DE VERGOR. The son of a former governor of Louisbourg, du Chambon was born in Placentia, Newfoundland, in 1712 and entered the army in 1737. He received an appointment to Canada in 1750. Du Chambon's capture that year by John Rous as he was taking a company of troops by sea from Québec to the River Saint John typifies the misfortune of his service. Under du Chambon's command, Fort Beauséjour was captured in 1755, and for this he was court martialed in 1757, but acquitted. Subsequently, he was stationed at Québec, and it was because of his lack of vigilance that Wolfe's forces were able to gain a foothold on the Plains of Abraham.

CHAUVREULX, ABBÉ CLAUDE-JEAN-BAPTISTE. In 1735, the Abbé Chauvreulx became the first resident priest among the Acadians of the Minas Basin. From 1749, he settled in the parish of Grand-Pré, where he ministered to more than 3,000 communicants. On the arrival of Cornwallis, he advised his parishioners to take the oath of allegiance discussed by Salusbury in the early pages of the journal and otherwise enjoyed good relations with the British. A month before the deportation of the Acadians in 1755, however, he was arrested by Lawrence, imprisoned in Fort Edward, and subsequently shipped back to France.

COBB, CAPTAIN SYLVANUS. Cobb was an accomplished soldier and sailor who was instrumental in protecting the coasts of Nova Scotia. Born in Plymouth, Massachusetts, in 1710, he was a captain in a Massachusetts regiment that took part in the siege of Louisbourg in 1745; afterwards he served there on garrison duty. More important, he was hired by Governor Cornwallis in January 1750 to sail his sloop *York* as part of the "sea militia" headed by Rous that patrolled the coasts of Nova Scotia for the next decade.

COLLIER, JOHN. Commissioned in the earl of Halifax's regiment, Collier had retired from the army when he arrived in Halifax with Governor Cornwallis in 1749. He was then named a justice of the peace and, enjoying the respect of Cornwallis, was appointed to the council in 1752. The following year, Collier succeeded Green as judge of the Court of Vice Admiralty and succeeded Salusbury as register and receiver of rents. As captain of one of the five companies of militia, he had one of the five divisions of the town named after him. His most outstanding contribution to the colony was made over the next twenty years in the administration of justice, sometimes contrary to the governor's wishes, and particularly during the Seven Years' War, when he acted as presiding judge of the Court of Vice Admiralty.

COPE, JEAN–BAPTISTE. "Major" Cope, as he was sometimes called, played an important part in the war between the Micmacs and the British from 1749 to 1753 as chief of the tribe of Shubenacadie. Though an ally of Abbé Le Loutre, he signed a treaty that Salusbury describes as "a foolish peice of formality" in November 1752, because by the following summer both sides had begun hostilities again.

CORNWALLIS, GOVERNOR EDWARD. The establishment of the settlement at Halifax was probably the most outstanding achievement of Edward Cornwallis. The son of a distinguished aristocratic family and the twin brother of a future archbishop of Canterbury, Cornwallis was only thirty-six when became governor of Nova Scotia and steered the colony through the precarious first two years. He had been commissioned in the army in 1731, but by a series of reversals he was forced to resign in 1748. Cornwallis was prudent and hard working during the two years in Halifax, though he admitted he had no head for the business problems he faced. He asked to be relieved after this time because he was plagued by severe bouts of rheumatism and, in spite of his efforts, was distressed by the treatment he received from the Board of Trade. The remainder of his long career was marred by one misfortune after another. In 1753, he was returned as member of Parliament for Westminster and the same year married the daughter of Viscount Townshend, who died in 1755. He shared part of the public odium resulting from the capitulation of Minorca in 1756. Perhaps because of his good connections at court, he always seemed to survive catastrophe and was eventually appointed governor of Gibraltar, with the rank of lieutenant-general, in 1762. He died in Gibraltar in 1776.

CRANE, REVEREND DOCTOR EDWARD. Dr. Crane was Salusbury's chief mentor and guide throughout his later life. Educated at Cambridge, he was raised to the priesthood in 1721 and received the LL.D. (*comitia regia*) in 1728. He had been Lord Halifax's tutor and was thus an integral part of the Halifax household when he was appointed prebend of Westminster in 1748. When Halifax was made lord lieutenant of Ireland, Crane was made his senior chaplain. Richard Cumberland writes that he subsequently declined the Irish bishopric of Elphin, preferring to return to the cloisters of Westminister. Afterwards Crane spent his declining years in a parsonage at Sutton, where he slowly died of cancer of the face.

FOYE, CAPTAIN WILLIAM. Foye was a prominent New Englander who arrived in Halifax with Cornwallis's convoy aboard the *Canning*. He was born in Boston in 1716, the son of William Foye, the treasurer and receiver general of Massachusetts, 1736–59, from whom he subsequently inherited valuable Boston properties. A graduate of Harvard, he had served in New England as a lieutenant and is listed as captain of an independent company on his arrival in Halifax. Cornwallis appointed him provost marshal in 1749, and he held this position until he died in 1771. Foye served as a member of the Legislative Assembly in 1758–59 and held the rank of lieutenant–colonel in the Halifax County militia in 1762.

GATES, CAPTAIN HORATIO. Gates was born in England in 1728. He had served previously as an army officer in North America before coming to Halifax as one of Cornwallis's aides-de-camp in 1749. From that date, he fought in the campaign against the Indians, particularly with Lawrence at Chignecto, and enjoyed the friendship and respect of John Salusbury. He left for New York in 1754 and was active until the peace of 1763, when he bought an estate in Virgina. At the beginning of the American Revolution, he offered his services to the Americans, took command of the Northern Army in 1777, and was victorious at Saratoga, eventually becoming a brigadier-general. He died in New York in 1806.

GILMAN, MAJOR EZEKIEL. As an army officer, Gilman had fought at Louisbourg in 1745 and was in England when the Board of Trade was fitting out the Nova Scotia settlers. He applied to the board as one skilled in erecting sawmills and laying out settlements, whereupon he was taken on for that purpose at ten shillings per day. The mill was an essential part of the new settlement since it provided necessary building supplies for new houses. During the first year, Gilman proceeded to set up his sawmill in Dartmouth, but because of the lack of protection there he was attacked by

Micmac Indians. Cornwallis thought Gilman managed the mill badly and dismissed him, next using him in the war against the Indians. In the summer of 1750, the sawmill passed into the hands of a Mr. Clapham. When it was sold at auction in 1752, Gilman, by now a civilian, bought it back.

GORHAM, COLONEL JOHN. As Sylvanus Cobb dominated the sea, John Gorham, with his company of rangers, contributed much to the maintenance of security ashore during the early years of the Halifax colony. Born in Massachusetts in 1709, the son of Colonel Shobal Gorham, he was first a merchant but became a militia captain in 1744 when he arrived to reinforce Annapolis Royal with a company of rangers. At Louisbourg in 1745, he served as a lieutenant-colonel in the Seventh Massachusetts Regiment under his father; on the death of his father at Louisbourg Gorham was promoted to full colonel (though in Nova Scotia he was styled "captain"). For the next several years, he fought throughout Nova Scotia at the head of his rangers. When Cornwallis arrived, Gorham was one of the first council members appointed. He established Fort Sackville in Bedford Basin and was involved in numerous skirmishes with the Indians for the next two years. In 1751, he accompanied John Salusbury home to England and died of smallpox in London a few months later.

GORHAM, JOSEPH. John Gorham's younger brother was born in Massachusetts in 1725. He served at both sieges of Louisbourg and received a commission in his brother's company of rangers in 1749. In this position, he exerted some influence over the Micmacs for the next ten years. He served at Québec in 1759, became governor of Placentia in 1770 and held the rank of major-general in the British army when he died in 1790.

GREEN, BENJAMIN. Born in Massachusetts in 1713, the youngest son of the rector of Salem, Benjamin Green reputedly became a merchant in Boston with his brothers before distinguishing himself, from 1745, as a colonial administrator at Louisbourg, first as Pepperrell's secretary and then as secretary to council. When he arrived in Halifax in 1749, he was made naval officer of the port and a member of council by Cornwallis. After the dismissal of Hugh Davidson in 1750, he became secretary and provincial treasurer. In addition, he served as a judge of both the Vice Admiralty Court and the Inferior Court of Common Pleas and thus for a decade was one of the most powerful men in Halifax. As such, he was suspected by John Salusbury of using his positions for his own aggrandizement and gain. He resigned as secretary in 1752 and as a judge of Vice Admiralty in 1753 but kept all his other appointments. While helping with the audit of Governor Hopson's accounts in England in 1762, he was found guilty by the Board of Trade of letting government contracts for his own profit; however, he was allowed to continue in office. Following his death in 1772, the auditors of his accounts found other irregularities that substantiated the suspicions of John Salusbury many years before.

HALIFAX, GEORGE MONTAGU DUNK, THIRD EARL OF. Lord Halifax was the only son of the second earl, whom he succeeded in 1739. The title did not bring him wealth, however, and in 1741 he married Miss Anne Dunk, a rich heiress, and thereafter he adopted her family name in addition to his own. Created a colonel in the army in 1745, he achieved the rank of lieutenant-general without ever engaging in combat. After a brief spell in opposition, he joined the government side and held cabinet positions under Grenville and Bute that included first lord of the Admiralty, secretary of state and lord privy seal before he died in 1771. Perhaps his greatest achievement was the development of the British mercantile interests in America, which he supervised as head of the Board of Trade and Plantations from 1748 until 1761. This period corresponds almost exactly with his acquaintance with John Salusbury, whose patron he was during Salusbury's service in Nova Scotia.

HAMILTON, JOHN. Hamilton was probably born at Annapolis, where his father, then Major Otho Hamilton, later governor of Placentia, was a member of council from 1731 to 1744. John Hamilton was married there to Mary Handfield, the daughter of a fellow officer (q.v.). On the arrival of Cornwallis, he was a lieutenant in the Fortieth Regiment, and in the incident described by Salusbury, he and a party of eighteen men detached by Handfield from the fort at Minas were attacked by about 300 Micmacs. Hamilton is not mentioned by Salusbury for more than two years while he and his men are held prisoners at Québec until the autumn of 1751, when they are ransomed by Cornwallis. Hamilton was also something of an artist, and he has left valuable sketches of British forts at Annapolis, the Minas Basin and Chignecto.

HANDFIELD, JOHN. Handfield was an officer in the Fortieth Regiment and from 1720 spent his entire military career in Nova Scotia. He was a member of the council at Annapolis for thirteen years and married a daughter of the mercantile Winniett family. In the autumn of 1749, he was dispatched with a contingent to protect the Minas area, and Salusbury visited his fort there during the expedition to Chignecto in 1750. Handfield later became commandant at Annapolis and was responsible for embarking the Acadians in that district in 1755. He later reached the rank of lieutenant-colonel and fought at the capture of Louisbourg in 1758.

HINCHELWOOD, ARCHIBALD. Hinchelwood had been a secretary at the War Office and an officer in the Twentieth Regiment when he embarked with Cornwallis in 1749 as his clerk. He then served in the secretary's office until 1756, when he was made deputy secretary. He represented Lunenburg in the assembly from 1759 until his death and was nominated to the council in 1773, but died that year before taking his seat.

HOPSON, GOVERNOR PEREGRINE. When Peregrine Hopson arrived in Halifax in July 1749, he had already had a full career as an army officer. As governor of Louisbourg, he had just completed negotiations for passing over the fortress to the French. Though he was soon sworn in as a member of the Halifax council, he returned to England that same summer and did not return until 1752, when he sailed to Halifax with Salusbury to relieve Cornwallis as governor. Salusbury grew to hate him, perhaps because of his more conciliatory attitude towards the Acadians and the Indians and his habit of "trimming" as he dealt with the rival British and New England factions in the town. As Salusbury was about to leave the second time, Hopson was launching the settlement of the "foreign Protestants" at Lunenburg. A few months after Salusbury's departure, Hopson too returned to England with eye trouble. He was promoted to major-general in 1757 and was still active as an officer when he died in 1758.

HOW, EDWARD. Edward How was a New Englander who began his career in Nova Scotia as a merchant in the Canso area around 1722. He became a member of council at Annapolis in 1736. His second wife was a member of the mercantile Winniett family. While commissary at Grand Pré in 1747, he was wounded during a French attack and taken prisoner, though he was later exchanged for six Frenchmen. With the arrival of Cornwallis, How was immediately appointed to the Halifax council. Because of How's familiarity with the Indians and the French in the Bay of Fundy area, Cornwallis used him to ratify the treaty with the Indians in 1749, and he was commissary of the second Chignecto expedition of 1750. On 4 October, while he was returning from a meeting with the French on the banks of the Missiguash River under a flag of truce, he was fired on from ambush and killed.

JONQUIÈRE, JACQUES PIERRE DE TAFFANEL, MARQUIS DE LA. The career of the Marquis de la Jonquière, governor of Canada, parallels almost exactly that of his counterpart Cornwallis. He had served as third in command of the magnificent fleet of the Duc d'Anville, which had failed to attack British America in 1746 because of heavy weather, and was captured the following year when a fleet under his own command was defeated by Anson and Warren. In August 1749, he became governor of Canada and died at Québec in 1752 at the age of sixty-seven.

LA CORNE, LOUIS DE. The "Chevalier de la Corne" was born at Fort Frontenac in 1703 and received a commission in the army in 1738. He came to the attention of Salusbury during the expedition to Chignecto of April 1750, when he was encountered, in conjunction with the Abbé Le Loutre, persuading French inhabitants to move across to the French side of the Missaguash River. Because of his overpowering numbers, he forced Charles Lawrence to withdraw on this occasion and was still in place there when Lawrence returned in September to erect Fort Lawrence.

LAWRENCE, GOVERNOR CHARLES. When Charles Lawrence came to Halifax in the autumn of 1749, he had already had twenty years' service in the army, including two at Louisbourg as a major in the Forty-fifth Regiment. From that time onward, he became perhaps the most distinguished soldier in Nova Scotia. From the time of his arrival, it seems, he established a friendship with John Salusbury that lasted through the rest of Salusbury's time in the colony, for both men enjoyed the patronage of the earl of Halifax. Salusbury frequently mentions his evenings with Lawrence in the early years and his correspondence with him while he was erecting Fort Lawrence. Perhaps for this reason, he accompanied Lawrence on the first expedition to Chignecto. When Lawrence returned from Chignecto the second time, he was a lieutenant-colonel. He was appointed by Governor Hopson to supervise the settlement of the "foreign Protestants" at Lunenburg in 1753, and that year, when Hopson returned to England because of ill health, Lawrence presided over the council. In 1756, he became governor. Meanwhile, he was directly responsible for carrying out the expulsion of the Acadians, an operation that has subsequently been condemned as harsh and unimaginative. Lawrence commanded a brigade at the second siege of Louisbourg in 1758 and the same year preoccupied himself with plans for a Nova Scotia assembly, which held its first meeting in October 1758. He died suddenly two years later from the effects of a chill.

LE LOUTRE, ABBÉ LOUIS JOSEPH DE. The Abbé Le Loutre, French missionary to the Micmacs from around 1740, was directly responsible for perpetrating acts of treachery against the British in Nova Scotia. He was able to do this by using funds and supplies of firearms from the government at Québec. In the early days of the Halifax settlement, his headquarters was established at Missiguash, where he encountered Lawrence on the first expedition to Chignecto and where, it is said, he planned and carried out the assassination of Edward How during a supposedly friendly meeting. He left Fort Beauséjour in 1755 before it surrendered to Monckton, but as he was sailing to France from Québec, the British captured his ship. Le Loutre was taken prisoner and confined on the island of Jersey until 1763.

LITTLE, OTIS. Otis Little was born to a prominent Massachusetts family in 1712. Educated at Harvard College and trained as a lawyer, he saw early service in the Annapolis area as a magistrate. In 1744 he was captured by the French as he led a company of volunteers. Little was interested in the eventual settlement of Nova Scotia, and his ideas are set forth in his pamphlet *The State of Trade in the Northern Colonies Considered* (1748). He went to London in 1746 seeking employment and returned with Cornwallis in 1749 as surveyor-general, advocate general of the Vice Admiralty Court and commissary of stores. From this last position he was suspended by Cornwallis in 1751 when his books were not found to be in order. Salusbury claims that he took up where Davidson had left off in selling stores for his own benefit. In 1753, he was found guilty of accepting bribes as a public prosecutor and stripped of his positions.

MAILLARD, ABBÉ PIERRE. Abbé Maillard was a confrere of Abbé Le Loutre as a French missionary in Nova Scotia, but in his attitude to the British and his sense of purpose he was quite the opposite. From the time of his arrival at

Ile Royale in 1735, he began to study the Micmac language and with his unusual linguistic abilities succeeded, in a few months, in not only mastering Micmac but devising a system for transcribing the words. This facility of language made him invaluable not only as a missionary but as a potential military asset, and prior to the arrival of Cornwallis he was engaged in assisting the Micmacs to support the French. He remained at Louisbourg until its fall in 1758, when he found himself deserted by the French in Nova Scotia. Around 1760, he accepted the invitation of Governor Lawrence to assist the British authorities in the pacification of the Micmacs and functioned as a British official at a salary of £150 until his death in 1762.

MASCARENE, PAUL. Paul Mascarene was born in France of Huguenot stock and arrived for the first time in North America with a British force in 1709. He was at Port-Royal at the surrender in 1710. The balance of his career was spent in Nova Scotia and New England. He became a lieutenant-colonel in the Fortieth Regiment in 1742 and as a senior officer at Annapolis, he administered the council there. When Cornwallis arrived, Mascarene was immediately sworn in as a member of council, but he returned to Annapolis that summer, and it was there that Salusbury met him on his return form Chignecto in 1750. Cornwallis sent the aging colonel to New England in 1751 to renew an Indian treaty, and this time he did not return. He spent his later years in Boston with his family and died there in 1760.

MONCKTON, ROBERT. Monckton was born in 1726, the second son of the first Viscount Galway, and was commissioned in the army at the age of fifteen. Having seen considerable action in Europe, in 1751 he became both a lieutenant-colonel in the Forty-seventh Regiment and, on the death of his father, member of Parliament for Pontefract. The following year, he joined his regiment, which had been sent to Nova Scotia the year before, and in August he was dispatched to relieve Charles Lawrence as commander of the fort at Chignecto. Monckton was sent to put down an armed insurrection in Lunenburg in 1753 and in 1755 returned to Chignecto in command when British forces finally reduced Fort Beauséjour. That year he was appointed lieutenant-governor of Nova Scotia. He returned to the army in 1758 to command an expedition to the Saint John River area and then was chosen by General Wolfe to be second in command of the Québec campaign the following summer. He subsequently became governor of New York, captured Martinique, and served again in Parliament until his death in 1782.

MONK, JAMES. James Monk was born in Wales and educated at Eton College but emigrated to Boston in 1736 to become a merchant. He accompanied Pepperrell to Louisbourg in 1745 as aide-de-camp and seems to have remained there until 1749. Cornwallis appointed him assistant surveyor in Halifax. He was also appointed a justice of the Inferior Court of Common Pleas in 1752 and survived the complaints of the merchants' group that year. In April, however, he was accused of defrauding a settler, Thomas Power, of land and was reprimanded by council. For the next several years, he seems to have been out of favor in Halifax until Lawrence appointed him solicitor general in 1760.

MOREAU, REVEREND JEAN-BAPTISTE. Moreau had been a French Roman Catholic priest before he emigrated to England and became an Anglican. He came to Nova Scotia as a settler with Cornwallis and soon afterwards the Society for the Propagation of the Gospel made him an assistant to their missionary, Tutty. Until 1753, he remained in Halifax, ministering chiefly to French-speaking Protestants, and in June of that year accompanied them to Lunenburg, where he remained as the only clergyman until 1761.

MORRIS, CHARLES. Charles Morris was a practical surveyor born in New England. In 1745, Governor William Shirley of Massachusetts directed him to make a survey of Nova Scotia that would serve as a basis for considering the colonization of the area (B.L. Add. MS 15,494, f.6). With Brewse, the military engineer, he laid out the town of Halifax. He was the first surveyor general, a judge of the Inferior Court of Common Pleas, and a member of council from 1755. From 1776 to 1778 he was chief justice of the Supreme Court.

NESBITT, WILLIAM. Nesbitt was a government clerk when he arrived in Nova Scotia with Cornwallis and served, in conjunction with Hinchelwood, in the secretary's office. He later practiced law before succeeding Little as attorney general. At the first general election in 1758, he was elected a representative for Halifax County and was speaker of the assembly from 1759 to 1783. He died the following year.

OSBORN, SIR DANVERS. Sir Danvers Osborn led a rather peripatetic life after his wife of three years, a sister of Lord Halifax, died in 1743. Probably it was Lord Halifax who influenced him to go to Nova Scotia in 1750. There he became a member of council, but after only six weeks he returned to England and testified before the Board of Trade on financial matters in the colony, notably the affair of Hugh Davidson. In 1753, the Board recommended him as governor of New York. Two days after he took up his appointment, he hanged himself.

PROCTOR, CHARLES. Proctor served as an officer at Louisbourg before coming to Halifax in 1749. He was commissioned to lay out the Halifax dockyard in 1758 and later became a surveyor of highways and a justice of the peace. He was an elected member of the assembly from 1759 to 1773.

ROUS, CAPTAIN JOHN. John Rous was the foremost New England privateer captain in the years preceding the founding of Halifax and was second in command of the Massachusetts naval forces at Louisbourg. As captain of the sloop *Albany*, he led the convoy of settlers to Halifax in 1749, and as senior naval officer he was involved in all major operations to preserve the new colony, notably the operation to Chignecto described by Salusbury. Until 1755, he had at his disposal only three fourteen-gun sloops. He commanded the naval force sent to capture Fort Beauséjour and was captain of a vessel that took part in the second siege of Louisbourg. A squadron under his command sailed past Québec in 1759 and landed troops for the assault. A year later, he died at Portsmouth, England.

SAUL, THOMAS. As the agent for the government contractor William Baker, Thomas Saul was one of the most influential men serving in an unofficial position in the early years of the settlement. Baker possessed a contract to victual and pay troops, and Saul's job was to supervise the arrangements. In view of the many financial problems encountered by Cornwallis during this period, Saul must have been one of the few people with access to both provisions and cash, and thus he was necessary to the survival of the colony. More than once Saul eased Cornwallis out of awkward situations at great profit to Baker. Eventually he was appointed commissary of stores and provisions. At the same time, Saul became a wealthy merchant, perhaps from following a well–established practice of trading with government stores; but although the Board of Trade was suspicious, he was never convicted of an offense, and he served in Halifax until 1760.

TUTTY, REVEREND WILLIAM. Tutty had only been ordained a priest for one year when he set out with Cornwallis as chaplain to the expedition. He held the first church services in Halifax aboard the *Beaufort* and later in the governor's dining room before preaching the first sermon in Saint Paul's. As the chief representative of the Established Church, Tutty soon lost the services of the bibulous Anwyl (q.v.) but found a replacement in Jean-Baptiste Moreau. From the beginning, Tutty complained of a pain in his side. He applied for permission to return to England to marry and when permission was finally granted in October 1752, he was succeeded oy Breynton. But although he married and became a father, he died in 1754, presumably of the affliction mentioned in his letters.

ZOUBERBUHLER, SEBASTIAN. One of those settlers whom John Salusbury quickly suspected of questionable practices was Sebastian Zouberbuhler, and though Salusbury only hints that he was mismanaging supplies allocated to the "foreign Protestants," Zouberbuhler's career shows the cause of Salusbury's suspicions. Born probably in Switzerland ca. 1710, he was involved in land speculation in South Carolina and Massachusetts in the 1730s and was found guilty, with Samuel Waldo, of neglecting German Protestants in Massachusetts in 1743. He fought in Waldo's regiment at Louisbourg in 1745, became a merchant there, and acted as the representative of Joshua Mauger. Perhaps because he could speak French and German, Zouberbuhler shrewdly became an agent for dealing with the "foreign Protestants" and in 1753 was sent as a magistrate to the new settlement at Lunenburg. He was subsequently elected to the provincial assembly, became a member of council in 1763 and acquired large grants of land during the land boom of 1765. He died in Lunenburg in 1773.

Notes

Introduction

1. *Speech of Edmund Burke, Esq* . . . . (London, 1780), p.76.

2. See Archibald M. MacMechan, ed., *Original Minutes of His Majesty's Council at Annapolis Royal, 1720–1736* (Halifax: McAlpine Publishing Co., 1908) and C. Bruce Fergusson, ed., *Minutes of His Majesty's Council at Annapolis Royal, 1736–1749* (Halifax: Public Archives of Nova Scotia, 1967).

3. See Max Savelle, *The Diplomatic History of the Canadian Boundary, 1749–1763* (New Haven, Conn.: Yale University Press, 1940), and N. E. S. Griffiths, "The Acadians," in *Dictionary of Canadian Biography*, 4 (1979), xvii–xxxi.

4. See *The Memorials of the English and French Commissaries Concerning the Limits of Nova Scotia or Acadia* (London, 1755).

5. See James A. Henretta, *"Salutary Neglect": Colonial Administration Under the Duke of Newcastle* (Princeton, N.J.: Princeton University Press, 1972), pp. 282–93, and George A. Rawlyk, *Nova Scotia's Massachusetts* (Montreal: McGill-Queen's Press, 1973), ch. 10.

6. "Extract of a Plan presented to His Majesty by the Earl of Halifax for the Settlement of His Majesty's Colony of Nova Scotia," *Report of the Board of Trustees of the Public Archives of Nova Scotia* (Halifax: Public Archives of Nova Scotia, 1971), Appendix B, p.29.

7. See especially the *Gentleman's Magazine* and the *Literary Magazine.*

8. "Nova Scotia. A New Ballad. To the Tune of King John

and the Abbot of Canterbury," *Gentleman's Magazine* 20 (1750): 84.

9. "The Weavers Wives Resolution, not to go to Nova Scotia," *The Nova Scotia's Garland; Furnished with Three merry New Songs* (Newcastle, ?1750), p.3.

10. "An Invitation to the famous and plentiful Island of Pleasure, call'd, New Scotland, in the Northern Parts of America," *The Nova Scotia's Garland*, p.7.

11. An interesting fictional reconstruction of these early days is Thomas Raddall's *Roger Sudden* (Toronto: McClelland, 1944).

12. "Copy of a Letter from one of the Settlers in Nova Scotia to his Friend in London, dated at Chibucto Harbour, July 28, 1749," *London Magazine* 18 (1749): 414.

13. "Extract of a Letter from a Gentleman at Chebucto in Nova Scotia, to his Father, dated August 19," *London Magazine* 18 (1749): 471.

14. CO 217/9, f. 70: Cornwallis to Board of Trade, 24 July 1749.

15. Reports of the Society for the Propagation of the Gospel, B. 17, 5: 17 March 1750.

16. From a letter dated 7 December 1749, *Gentleman's Magazine* 20 (1750): 73.

17. PRO 30/50/39, f. 30: Davidson to Richard Aldworth, 19 October 1949.

18. See George T. Bates, "The Great Exodus of 1749, or, the Cornwallis Settlers Who Didn't," *Collections of the Nova Scotia Historical Society* 38 (1973): 27–62.

19. *Journal of the Commissioners for Trade and Plantations* (London: HM Stationery Office, 1936), 9: 3.

20. Reports of the Society for the Propagation of the Gospel, B. 17, 22: 29 September 1749.

21. PRO 30/50/39, f. 29: Davidson to Aldworth, 19 October 1749.

22. See T. B. Akins, "The First Council," *Collections of the Nova Scotia Historical Society* 2 (1881): 17–30.

23. CO 217/9, f. 85: List of civil officers.

24. PRO 30/50/39, f. 29: Davidson to Aldworth, 19 October 1749.

25. Professor J. G. Adshead unravels the confusion over JS's birth date in "Hon. John Salusbury, 1707-62," *Collections of the Nova Scotia Historical Society* 29 (1951): 6-7.

26. Hester Lynch Piozzi, *Thraliana: The Diary of Mrs. Hester Lynch Thrale (Later Mrs. Piozzi)*, ed. Katherine C. Balderston (Oxford: Clarendon Press, 1951), 1:284-85.

27. Richard Cumberland, *Memoirs* (London, 1806), p.100.

28. See A. H. Basye, *The Lords Commissioners of Trade and Plantations* (New Haven, Conn.: Yale University Press, 1925), pp.81-82.

29. Rylands Eng. MS 530, no. 51: Crane to JS, 15 June 1749.

30. Rylands Eng. MS 530, no. 54: Halifax to JS, 18 October 1749.

31. Ibid.

32. I rely for genealogical details and personal recollections of the Salusburys and Cottons on John Salusbury's daughter, Hester, in *Thraliana*, 1:275-304. Sir John Ballinger gives a complete account of Salusbury ancestry in "Kathryn of Berain," *Y Cymmroder* 40 (1929): 1-42; extensive biographical information about Sir John Salusbury of Lleweni (ca. 1566-1612), the poet, appears in the introduction to *Poems of Sir John Salusbury and Robert Chester*, ed. Carleton Brown (London, 1914); the introduction and three genealogical tables in the *Calendar of Salusbury Correspondence, 1553-circa 1700*, ed. W. J. Smith (Cardiff: University of Wales Press, 1954), pursues in some detail the rise of the Salusburys and I am indebted to the summary of the family's history provided by James L. Clifford in the first two chapters of *Hester Lynch Piozzi (Mrs. Thrale)* (Oxford: Clarendon Press, 1952).

33. Clifford, *Hester Lynch Piozzi*, p. 5, n. 2.

34. Balderston, ed., *Thraliana*, 1:276, n. 5.

35. Probably this school was connected with the old Whitchurch, Denbigh.

36. John Venn and J. A. Venn, *Alumni Cantabrigienses* (Cambridge: University Press, 1922-54), Part 1, 4, 7.

37. Balderston, ed., *Thraliana*, 1:276.

38. Ibid., p.277.

39. Ibid., p.279.

40. Rylands Charters 1231 and 1232.

41. Rylands Charter 1008.

42. Rylands Eng. MS 530, no. 60.

43. See photograph in Mary Hyde, *The Thrales of Streatham Park* (Cambridge, Mass.: Harvard University Press, 1977), p.3.

44. Balderston, ed., *Thraliana*, 1:281.

45. Ibid.

46. Ibid., p.282 and n.4.

47. Ibid., p.284.

48. Ibid., p.285, and G. E. C. Cokayne, ed., *Complete Baronetage* (Exeter: W. Pollard and Co., 1900–06), 4:84.

49. Hester Lynch Piozzi, *Dr. Johnson's Mrs. Thrale*, ed. A. Hayward and J. H. Lobban (Edinburgh: T. N. Foulis, 1910), p.7.

50. Rylands Eng. MS 531, f. 2: Bridge to JS, 23 April 1749.

51. Rylands Eng. MS 530, 52: Crane to JS, 28 September 1750.

52. Rylands Eng. MS 530, 56: Collier to JS, 29 September 1753.

53. I have examined Salusbury's Halifax holdings and his daughter's attempts to repossess them in "Mrs. Hester Thrale (Piozzi) and the Pursuit of her 'Nova Scotia Fortune'," *Dalhousie Review* 58 (1978): 434–42.

54. *Halifax Gazette*, 25 November 1752, p.2.

55. Balderston, ed., *Thraliana*, 1:293.

56. Ibid.

57. *Gentleman's Magazine* 22 (1752): 385.

58. CO 218/4, f. 220–21: Board of Trade to Hopson, 28 March 1753.

59. Balderston, ed., *Thraliana*, 1:294.

60. Ibid., p.290.

61. See engraving of Llewenny Hall and photograph of East Hyde in Hyde, *The Thrales of Streatham Park,* pp.94 and 5.

62. Balderston, ed., *Thraliana,* 1:290.

63. See engraving of Offley Place in Hyde, *The Thrales of Streatham Park*, p.78.

64. *Journal of the Commissioners for Trade and Plantations,* 9:77.

65. St. Paul's Church Register, vol. 1 passim.

66. Balderston, ed., *Thraliana*, 1:127.

67. Rylands Eng. MS 616: young Hetty's daily journal.

68. Balderston. ed., *Thraliana,* 1:263.

69. Piozzi, *Dr. Johnson's Mrs. Thrale*, p.311. Mrs. Piozzi writes to Sir James Fellowes, 30 October 1815, "My father and he were very intimate, and he often dined with us." Ronald Paulson notes in *Hogarth*: *His Life, Art, and Times* (New Haven, Conn.: Yale University Press, 1971), 2:291, "It is evident that he was a close friend of John Salusbury, her father, who was the only subscriber for *Sigismunda* (1761) to refuse the refund Hogarth offered when he failed to secure an engraver."

70. Balderston, ed., *Thraliana*, 1:296.

71. A. M. Broadley, *Doctor Johnson and Mrs. Thrale* (London: John Lane, 1910), p.105.

72. Balderston, ed., *Thraliana*, 1:298.

73. Ibid., pp.300–301.

74. Ibid., p.304. *Gentleman's Magazine* 32 (1762): 601, records his death for 18 December.

75. Rylands Eng. MS 530, 31: Halifax to Sir Thomas Salusbury, 23 December 1762.

76. Balderston, ed., *Thraliana*, 1:127.

77. Ibid., p.127.

78. Ibid., p.313.

79. See p. 31, n. 53.

80. *The Spectator*, ed. Donald F. Bond (Oxford: Clarendon Press, 1965), 3:156.

81. Rylands Eng. MS 530, 54: Halifax to JS, 18 October 1749. Halifax writes, "The Accounts you have given me of the Country give me a perfect Idea of it, and your Journal of Transactions is greatly satisfactory to me. pray continue it, & let me hear from you as often as you conveniently can."

82. J. W., *A Letter from a Gentleman in Nova-Scotia* (London, 1756), p.9.

83. *London Magazine* 18 (1749): 471.

84. A summary of British treaties with the Micmacs is provided by Elizabeth A. Hutton, "The Micmac Indians of Nova Scotia to 1834" (M.A. thesis, Dalhousie University, 1961), ch. 4.

85. *London Magazine* 18 (1749): 574.

86. *London Magazine* 20 (1751): 419.

87. Ibid., p.341. John Wilson, in *A Genuine Narrative of the Transactions in Nova Scotia* (London, 1751?), p.14, describes the scalping process this way: "These *Indians* chain the unfortunate Prisoner to a large thick Tree, and bind his Hands and his Feet, then beginning from the middle of the *Craneum*, they cut quite round towards the Neck; this being done, they then tear off the Skin, leaving the Skull bare; an Inflammation quickly follows, the Patient fevers, and dies in the most exquisite Tortures."

88. CO 217/9, f. 190: Cornwallis to Board of Trade, 19 March 1750.

89. ADM 51/4109, ff. 10–11.

90. British Library Add. MS 35,913, f.9: Cornwallis to Bedford, 1 May 1750.

91. See Lawrence's report in "A journal of the proceedings of the Detachment under the Command of Maj^r. Lawrence, after Entering the Bason of Chinecto [26 April 1750]," CO 217/10, f. 9 ff.

92. ADM 51/4109, ff. 27–30.

93. I am grateful to W.A.B. Douglas for bringing the following facts to my attention. They are examined in his authoritative work, "Nova Scotia and the Royal Navy, 1713–1766" (Ph.D. diss., Queen's University, 1973).

94. Ibid., ch. 6: "The Sea Militia of Nova Scotia, 1749–1755."

95. Extracts from public documents on finance during these years are provided in Adam Shortt, et al., eds., *Documents Relating to Currency, Exchange and Finance in Nova Scotia with Prefatory Documents, 1675–1758* (Ottawa: King's Printer, 1933), pp.280–404.

96. See especially CO 217/11, f. 6 ff.: Cornwallis to Board of Trade, 27 November 1750.

97. CO 217/14, f. 1: Petition of Lieutenant William Martin.

98. See W. T. Baxter, *The House of Hancock, Business in Boston 1724-1775* (New York: Russell and Russell, 1945), pp. 118-23.

99. *Journal of the Commissioners for Trade and Plantations*, 9:77—29 May 1750.

100. CO 221/28, passim, and Shortt, et al., *Documents*, pp.284-86: Martin to Cornwallis, 8 October 1751.

101. *Journal of the Commissioners for Trade and Plantations*, 9:43.

102. CO 218/3, ff. 131–42: Board of Trade to Cornwallis, 14 June 1750.

103. Shortt, et al., *Documents*, p. 295: 16 June 1750.

104. CO 217/10, ff. 5–6: Cornwallis to Board of Trade, 10 July 1750.

106. *Journal of the Commissioners for Trade and Plantations*, 9:143.

107. Ibid., 9:218.

108. For permission to use extensive details of Mauger's life, I am grateful to Donald F. Chard and the *Dictionary of Canadian Biography*.

109. In CO 217/14, ff. 30-34, Hopson to Board of Trade, 28 March 1753, Governor Hopson explains the causes and results of the trial.

110. CO 220/3, p. 83 ff.

111. Ibid., pp. 164–65.

112. Ibid., pp. 168–69.

Book 1

1. The first book is marked "2." Since Cornwallis arrived on 21 June, it appears that a first book has been lost.

2. Cornwallis's transport ships, mentioned in the following pages, were the following: *Alexander, Baltimore, Beaufort, Brotherhood, Canning, Charlton, Everley, Fair Lady, London, Merry Jacks. Roehampton, Wilmington, Winchelsea.*

3. Cf. CO 217/9, ff. 78–79. Three French deputies insisted

they had previously taken the oath on the condition that they should always be exempted from bearing arms. The council could find no such condition and sent them back to their departments with the oath, to return in a fortnight with the resolutions of the inhabitants. A discussion of Acadian reaction to the oath of allegiance is given in W. Peter Ward, "The Acadian Response to the Growth of British Power in North America, 1749–1755," *Dalhousie Review* 51 (1971): 165–77.

4. Probably Henry Cooley, a civilian at Annapolis working for King Gould, the Fortieth Regiment's agent in London. See Fortieth Regiment papers in PANS, especially MS 259, 286, and 287, 1738–50.

5. William Shirley, who planned the expedition against Louisbourg in 1745, was one of the commissioners for settling the limits of Acadia.

6. Cf. CO 217/9, f. 75 f., and *Albany* journal. Captain John Rous of the *Albany* sloop had been sent to find out whether a new fortification was being built at the mouth of the River St. John and to notify the commander that he was to abandon it.

7. Cf. CO 220/2, p.4. The following were appointed justices of the peace: John Brewse, Robert Ewer, John Collier, and John Duport.

8. Ibid., pp.4–5. The settlers were ordered to assemble the following day to elect constables, one for each ship's company.

9. Possibly William Lloyd, captain of the *Sphinx*, but more probably David Lloyd, clerk of the stores.

10. JS was not commissioned register until 7 August.

11. JS's manservant.

12. Indented sections appear on the left-hand page of the original.

13. Thomas Salusbury, JS's brother.

14. Hester Salusbury, JS's wife.

15. Hopson was sworn in as a member of council.

16. This would appear to be a trial before the council, who acted as the Supreme Court. Unfortunately the first pages of the Supreme Court records are missing. The first entries available begin with September 1749.

17. This was one of the rare occasions on which JS missed a council meeting. Colonel Robert Ellison and Colonel James F. Mercer were sworn in as councillors.

18. Joseph Gorham.

19. Cf. CO 217/9, f. 83. The deputies presented a letter purported to be the sentiments of the inhabitants, demanding free exercise of religion and exemption from bearing arms.

20. Hugh Davidson, secretary of the council?

21. Hugh Davidson?

22. A reference to the death of Queen Caroline in 1737 from a "rupture" of the navel. The queen's gigolo, Lord Hervey, relates that it was first perceived during the birth of one of her daughters. See Hervey, *Memoirs* (London: Eyre and Spottiswoode, 1931) 3:877–917.

23. Cf. ADM 6/17, f. 424. Charles Davids was lieutenant of the *Sphinx*.

24. Cf. PANS, RG 1, vol. 163, pp. 153–54. The council of war, consisting of Governor Cornwallis, Colonels Hopson, Horsman, Mascarene, Ellison, and Mercer and Major Charles Lawrence, met to regulate the pay and provisioning of the troops in the colony.

25. See "Project for Fortifying the Town of Halifax; in Nova Scotia. 1749. Jn°: Brewse," British Library, *King's Topographical Collection*, 119, f. 77.

26. Captain Robert Ewer, a justice of the peace and commander of one of the five companies of town militia.

27. Refers perhaps to Captain Robert Ewer's attendance at council.

28. See Winthrop P. Bell, *The "Foreign Protestants" and the Settlement of Nova Scotia* (Toronto: University of Toronto Press, 1961), pp. 403–4 et passim. Cornwallis is reputed to have discovered an Indian known as "Old Labrador" when he put in at Merligash before making his landfall at Chebucto.

29. William Martin?

30. How was proceeding to the camping ground of the St. John's Indians to obtain a ratification of the treaty, which he did on 4 September.

31. See JS's letter of 19 August. Captain Gorham and his rangers, with an armed sloop, had been sent to the head of Bedford Basin, where they were to establish themselves for the winter to control the basin and keep open communication with Annapolis via the small post at Minas.

32. Cobequid (later Truro).

33. Abbé Jacques Girard.

34. Probably Captain George Scott, later of the Fortieth Regiment.

35. Probably Lord Halifax, Dr. Edward Crane, and Thomas Salusbury.

36. David Lloyd.

37. See CO 217/9, f. 89. On 19 August, Indians took twenty prisoners at Canso, men from Halifax and Boston making hay. They were carried to Louisburg on 29 August and set free by Monsieur Des Herbiers, commandant at Louisbourg. See below, 2 September.

38. Joseph Gorham.

39. Perhaps Joseph L'Andrée, a French settler loyal to the British.

40. Otis Little.

41. Peter Carteel, a settler, was taken into custody for the murder of Abram Goodsides, a boatswain's mate in the *Beaufort*.

42. William Lloyd.

43. CO 217/9, f. 97 ff. JS was a member of council ordering the trial of Peter Carteel. The trial was held in an ordnance storehouse fitted up for the purpose.

44. Prince Edward Island.

45. Major Hungerford Luttrell of the Forty-fifth Regiment.

46. Ephraim Cooke.

47. In *Collections of the Nova Scotia Historical Society* 12 (1905), pp. 3–4, we find Governor Cornwallis suffered many attacks of acute rheumatism that confined him to bed half of the time. Perhaps as a consequence he returned to England in 1752. See also *An Essay on the Present State of the Province of Nova-Scotia* (London, ?1774).

48. JS's youngest brother, Henry, who because of an accident in his childhood was not of sound mind.
49. CO 217/9, f. 100. Executed by hanging.
50. Sir Lynch Salusbury Cotton.
51. Possibly John Gorham, a member of council whom Governor Cornwallis did not respect (see below, p. 78, n. 30).
52 *OED*. Cod. The inmost recess of a bay or inland sea.
53. Captain William Clapham, commander of a company of rangers ordered raised by Cornwallis on his arrival.
54. Trading vessel. See below, 22 September.
55. Captain John Handfield of the Fortieth Regiment.
56. Captain Benjamin Ives had served with Pepperrell at Louisbourg. He sailed to Halifax with Cornwallis and was appointed captain of the port.
57. Northwest Arm.
58. CO 220/2, pp. 16–17. Elijah Davies had sought satisfaction from Ephraim Cooke, who had cut off Davies's bowsprit in a collision. The umpire, Captain Rous, ordered Cooke to pay damages. But not only did Cooke refuse to comply with the order, he did not even carry out the courtesy of returning it to the governor's messenger. At this council meeting, he was ordered not to set foot on shore until he had asked the governor's pardon.
59. See 18 September.
60. Probably JS's friend Charles Lawrence.
61. Major Ezekiel Gilman.
62. Cf. *Literary Magazine* 18 (1749): 574.
63. CO 220/2, pp. 17–18. JS is mistaken. The council viewed a declaration of war as recognition of the Indians as a separate nation. Instead, they offered a premium of ten guineas for every Indian killed or taken prisoner and took other precautionary measures.
64. Orders given to Clapham and Gilman were passed at the council meeting on 1 October.
65. Perhaps Robert Grant, surgeon and later merchant.

Book 2

1. PANS, RG 1, vol. 491, pp. 1–4. Michael Hendly, seaman aboard Cooke's ship *Baltimore*, claimed non-payment of wages totalling £16 6*s* and the withholding of his bedding and clothes. Cooke was ordered to give it back and to pay court costs.
2. Merligash (later Lunenburg)?
3. Grant of land.
4. *OED*. Drive. To float along, drift.
5. Now part of Her Majesty's Canadian Dockyard.
6. Cape Sambro.
7. Piziquid (later Windsor).
8. See above, p. 67.
9. See below, p. 96 and n. 2.
10. Captain George St. Loe of the Fortieth Regiment.
11. Probably Davidson, Martin, and Delancy. See below.
12. Oliver DeLancy of the firm of Delancy and Watts, a brother of the chief justice of New York, was prominent in New York financial and business life.
13. John Wilson, however, does not agree. In *A Genuine Narrative of the Transactions in Nova Scotia . . .* (London, ?1751), p. 10, he writes, "Many unfortunate People died of Cold the first Winter after their Settlement. This indeed, may be imputed to the Want of Houses, which only such as could build were able to obtain; and to see the vast Flakes of Snow lying about the Tents of those who had been accustomed to warm Fires about *Newcastle* and *London*, was enough to move the Heart of Stone."
14. Probably Joshua Mauger, whose name is pronounced "major."
15. This would seem to support the view that the target of this nickname was John Gorham, who held the provincial rank of colonel but was given the rank of captain in Halifax.

16. The militia amounted to about 840 men between the ages of 16 and 60. Cornwallis remarked in CO 217/9, f. 189, "The officers behaved well. I cannot commend the behaviour of the men in general, notwithstanding the danger they imagined threatned them."

17. Actually, there were eighteen men.

18. See CO 219/3, ff. 2–13, "An Act for Erecting Courts of Judicature within the Province of Nova Scotia and for Regulating the Proceedings thereof, made and passed in Council at Halifax Decr. the 13th 1749." Most of these items were derived from the laws of Virginia by the committee, which was composed of JS, Davidson, and Green.

19. Later McNab's Island.

20. CO 217/9, f. 188. Cornwallis wrote on 19 March that she had been detained by a contrary wind.

21. As a merchant, Joshua Mauger had ships sailing regularly from Halifax.

22. Memoranda such as this refer to JS's personal funds, which he kept hidden at home.

23. These three were later released, for their fathers were working in Halifax. See George T. Bates, "The Great Exodus of 1749, or, the Cornwallis Settlers Who Didn't," *Collections of the Nova Scotia Historical Society* 38 (1973): 58.

24. CO 217/9, f. 189. The artificers formed a company of their own.

25. JS became a close friend of Captain Ewer. He was lodging at Ewer's house at this time.

26. Le Loutre.

27. Sir Lynch Salusbury Cotton became M.P. for Denbighshire on 5 December 1749 on the death of Sir Watkin Williams Wynn.

28. CO 217/9, f. 190. A priest and two deputies brought by Captain Francis Bartelo had been examined by the council.

29. CO 217/9, f. 190. Cornwallis had sent Cobb to Boston to arm and man his sloop.

30. JS suspects someone of informing the Indians, though he never names him. He may have suspected Mauger, who was in touch with the French and the Indians regularly through trade. Bartelo was sent to bring the priest and deputies from

Cobequid. Cornwallis wrote, CO 217/9, f. 190, "This Command I gave to Captain Bartelo, whom I could confide in as a good Officer & an honest man. Capt. Gorham is good for nothing, & had declared lately that it was impracticable to go to Cobequide—"

31. This is the first indication that JS was willing to give up his post. Through the influence of Lord Halifax, he hoped to have himself recalled to England.

32. JS suggests that Secretary Davidson was "engrossing," or buying up, stock in order to "regrate" it, or sell it at a monopoly price.

33. Chauvreulx.

34. When Cornwallis sent in January a messenger to Girard, the priest at Cobequid, Micmacs loyal to Le Loutre made him prisoner and sent him to Chignecto. The governor then sent a force of 100 men, but before they arrived the Indians fled, and the troops took only the priest and deputies as prisoners. Upon taking the oath of allegiance, they were released.

Book 3

1. The Feast of the Annunciation.

2. Captain Jeremiah Rogers of the *Ulysses*.

3. Rous had been given the sloops *Dove* and *York* to escort the convoy. See below, p. 81, and *Albany* lieutenant's journal, National Maritime Museum, Greenwich, ADM/L/A 65.

4. Joseph Burn was master of the schooner *Chance*.

5. CO 220/2, p. 46. The governor's opinion was that "it is absolutely Necessary to secure the Isthmus immediately if a Sufficient Force can Possibly be spared for that purpose."

6. Warburton's Regiment, the Forty-fifth Regiment of Foot.

Book 4

1. For a more discursive account of the siege, see *The Journal of Joshua Winslow*, ed. J. C. Webster (St. John, N. B.: New Brunswick Museum, 1926).

2. See *A Plan of the River Chibenaccadie from its Source*

to its Discharge into the Bay of Mines. Surveyed in August 1754, British Library, *King's Topographical Collection*, 119: 61-a, which traces the regular route and illustrates a number of the locations mentioned here.

3. JS comments on possible mineral deposits throughout Book 4, probably as a result of the governor's interest in the economic potential of the terrain as outlined in his commission (CO 218/3, f. 27 ff.). JS's letter of 17 July 1750 refers to this. The Board of Trade and Plantations discouraged the opening of a coal colliery since it would surely lead to the manufacture of goods that Britain was selling to the colonies (CO 218/4, f. 71). But in March 1750, the board noted that part of the unforeseen expenses of the colony had arisen because no limestone had been found locally (CO 218/4, f.5). This was badly needed for bricks. Thus, JS looked for limestone throughout the expedition and a search was also made in the Halifax area (CO 217/10, f. 5) to no avail. A more detailed and articulate description of the Minas area is given by Captain William Owen, R.N., in "Narrative—Voyages, Travels, &c," in the library of the National Maritime Museum, Greenwich, COO/1.

4. British Library, *King's Topographical Collection*, 119: 60, shows the French families in the area, one of which is named "Babin."

5. *OED*. Champion. Open, level plain.

6. The Conway River issues from the mountainous district of North Wales where the counties of Merioneth, Denbigh, and Carnarvon meet.

7. Probably the present location of Falmouth.

8. Rhuddlan, an ancient parliamentary borough and parish on the river Clwyd, about eight miles northwest of Denbigh. Between the town and the sea is Rhuddlan Marsh, where the Welsh under Caradoc were defeated in 795 by the Saxons under Offa, King of Mercia.

9. In fact, no mines had ever been started there.

10. Samuel Johnson, *A Dictionary of the English Language* (London, 1755). Air. Publication. Exposure to the publick view and knowledge.

11. Blomidon.

12. Perhaps Penrhyn-Darnddu, a hill near the village of Penrhyn Coch in Cardiganshire.

13. *Johnson*. Eligible. Preferable.

14. CO 221/28, f. 149. Robert Gordon and Co., the Annapolis agent at Boston, owned the sloop *Seaflower*. See also Archibald M. MacMechan, ed., *A Calendar of Two Letter-Books and One Commission-Book in the Possession of the Government of Nova Scotia, 1713–1741* (Halifax: Herald Printing House, 1900), passim.

15. JS probably suspects Davidson.

16. See W. A. Calnek, *History of the County of Annapolis* (Toronto: William Briggs, 1897). William Winniett, who died in 1741, had been a merchant at Annapolis Royal as early as 1721 trading with the French at Chignecto and Minas. He was succeeded by his sons.

17. Captain Phillips of the *Warren*.

18. *OED*. To make a head. To raise a body of troops.

19. Probably Mauger or Davidson.

20. According to the *Albany* journal, ff. 20–21, Rous was delayed by contrary tides in the Bay of Fundy, a serious challenge to seamen. Capt. Samuel Hood (later Admiral Lord Hood) wrote to Richard Grenville, "The Bay of Fundy is a very ugly and precarious navigation; it is indeed a very dangerous one in winter." See *The Grenville Papers*, ed. William James Smith (London: John Murray, 1852–53): 164; 22 September 1767.

21. Cf. *Albany* journal, ff. 10–11, and Major Lawrence's journal, CO 217/10.

22. Cape Fendu or Cape Split.

23. CO 221/29, f. 37. Nathan Miller was the owner of the schooner *Patience* of Newport, Rhode Island.

24. William Magee was a Halifax merchant.

25. A term used by officers to refer to the men.

26. Probably Partridge Island.

27. A seaport in southwest Carnarvonshire shut in on three sides by a semi-circular range of hills.

28. Probably Port Mills, now Lockport.

29. The Joggins outcroppings, which were visible from sea.

30. The disposition of the Landry family is shown in British Library, *King's Topographical Collection*, 119: 60. There were several settlers in this area with the name Landrée, as shown in B.L. Add. MS 19,071, f. 143 ff., a record of quit-rents paid by the Acadians. This particular settler might have been Joseph Landrée, who was loyal to the British and who after the explusion of the Acadians in 1755 settled at Cape Sable. See T. B. Akins, ed., *Selections from the Public Documents of the Province of Nova Scotia* (Halifax: C. Annand, 1869), pp. 306–7.

31. In the *Albany* journal, ff. 11–12, Rous reported, "finding the Enemy to be Superior to our N°: & raining Incessantly all that day & no place of Shelter for our forces. they thought proper to repair & Joyn me in the Road, and proceed back to Minas their to wait his Excellency Governor Cornwallis's orders."

32. Tan-y-Bwlch, a hamlet in Merioneth that had been long a favorite of Welsh tourists.

33. Cf. *The Journal of Joshua Winslow*, ed. Webster, p. 15: "April 28. Lt. Gorham went with a command on board the Dove, which sailed the same day, as did Mr. Salisbury, for Annapolis Royal."

34. Henry Brydges, 2d duke of Chandos, was a patentee for coal mines in Nova Scotia.

35. *Johnson.* Conjure. To conspire; to bind many by an oath to some common design. It is to be observed that when this word is used for *summon* or *conspire*, its accent is on the last syllable, conjùre; when for *charm,* on the first, cònjure.

36. JS apparently calls the present Brier Island "Long Island" and the present Long Island "Salusbury Island." The smaller of the two is also called "Long Island" in Charles Morris's "Chart of the Sea Coasts of the Peninsula of Nova Scotia . . . " (1755), British Library, *King's Topographical Collection*, 119, 58-a.

37. Cornwallis was originally bound for Annapolis (CO 217/9, f. 67), but having no pilot, he put into a convenient anchorage.

38. St. Margaret's Bay, perhaps a second anchorage. The two places are not close.

39. At the end of this book, a note perhaps in Dr. Johnson's hand states, "Read Every other Page and continues the Journal of the weather and some few Events. the other Remarks Occasionally &c."

Book 5

1. PANS, RG 1, vol. 163, pp. 39–40. Davidson was sent to consult Governor Phips about the dangers threatening the colony and to settle the method of furnishing stores and money.

2. This cloth had probably been sent by Hetty. Mrs. Thrale wrote in *Thraliana*, 1:292, "She had however out of the little She allowed herself saved a trifling Sum—to her a large one—half of which She laid out in finery for my Father to cut a figure at the King's Birthday in Nova Scotia, which she sent by a Ship that was lost."

3. This was a favorite Indian gathering place for hunting, fishing, and festivities. In May, on the seventh day after the first moon, occurred the Feast of Saint Aspinquid, named for an Indian missionary canonized for his efforts. See Thomas H. Raddall, "The Feast of St. Aspinquid," *Nova Scotia Historical Quarterly* 1 (1971): 1–9.

4. See CO 217/10, f. 56. Davidson wrote to Viscount Dupplin at the Board of Trade on 16 June, "I was extremely lucky that I came here, for the Governor had no money sent them, nor could have had for some weeks to come. I sent back the Sloop I came in the Thursday after my arrival with Dollars (6000) & tents which were greatly wanted & other things that were ready to be Shipp'd. I have drawn for about 900 £ S^t.

5. This probably refers to the Indian attack on Dartmouth on 27 May. Details are given by Wilson, *A Genuine Narrative of the Transactions in Nova Scotia*, pp. 15–20.

6. Probably Lieutenant William Martin, who worked in conjunction with Davidson at Boston.

7. Martin.

8. The monkey in Gay's *Fables*. In Fable 14, a monkey resolves to leave his natural habitat, allows himself to be ensnared, and is made a pet by a lady who keeps him chained in her room. Here, by observation, he learns all the courtly graces. Eventually, he breaks free and returns to the woods, where his fellow monkeys admire his manner and dress and he advises them on behavior.

9. *Trial* and *Hound*.

10. CO 217/10, f. 7, Cornwallis to Board of Trade, 10 July 1750: "Lord Colvill in His Majesty's Ship Success hearing there was no Man of War here, came in last Week in his return from Louisburg." According to the ship's log (ADM 51, 940, Part I) the ship was anchored 4 July to 8 August. Alexander, seventh Baron Colvill, was commander of the *Success* on the North American station from 1749 to 1752.

11. JS was one of three, including Benjamin Green and William Steele, who submitted their report on 20 September 1750 (CO 217/10, ff. 68–76). Suspicions against Davidson were expressed in a Board of Trade letter of 14 June 1750 (CO 218/3, ff. 131–42) and a charge was made against him on 9 November 1750 (CO 218/3, ff. 147–52). See also JS's letter of 20 September.

12. Lieutenant John Hussey of the Forty-seventh Regiment, who was commander of Fort Lawrence in 1754 and was killed at the battle of Ste. Foy in 1760.

13. JS's schooner, named after Lord Halifax's family name.

14. The Fortieth Regiment, formerly Phillips's Regiment, of which Cornwallis was made colonel on 13 March 1750.

15. Forty-seventh Regiment of Foot.

16. See CO 217/40, ff. 285–86. At a council meeting of 25 September 1750, Cornwallis proposed to the Halifax merchants that he issue his own certificates of credit or issue bills of exchange for £50, providing one-fourth was paid in dollars. When the merchants did not agree, the plan was dropped.

17. According to the *Albany* journals, they sailed on 15 August with seven transports.

18. *OED*. Shallop. A boat, propelled by oars or by sail, for

use in shallow water or as a means of effecting communication between, or landings from, vessels of a large size, a dinghy.

19. The *Albany* journal shows that she took on troops on 31 August.

20. Webster, ed., *The Journal of Joshua Winslow*: "Mr Breuse the Engineer who attended him was wounded above the Knee but is in way of recovery."

21. CO 217/11, f. 3, Cornwallis to Board of Trade, 27 November 1750.

22. CO 217/10, f. 63 f., Cornwallis to Board of Trade, 16 September 1750.

23. *Johnson*. Jack. Used as a general term of contempt for saucy or paltry fellows.

24. Perhaps a reference to the collection of Scots in Halifax mercantile affairs that included Davidson, Gordon, Campbell, and Magee.

25. There was a direct route from the St. Lawrence to the mouth of the St. John River. See map drawn by Ensign James Peachey of the Sixtieth Regiment, British Library, *King's Topographical Collection*, 119: 59-2-c.

26. 30 October.

27. De Vergor du Chambon.

28. On 6 October, Rous fought the brig and schooner from 2 P.M. to 7 P.M. before capturing the brig. He reported in the *Albany* journal, ff. 31–32, that "she proved to be the S^t^. Francis Briggantine Commanded by Mons^re^. Vergo De Chamboug Commandant of a french Company of Troops, Came from Quebec bound to the River St. Johns in the Bay of fundy & Loaden with provisions, Stores, & Merchandize for his Majesty's Enemies, the Indians, at that fort, as was also the Schooner her Consort, & who dureing the Engagement made their Escape; The Brigg being about 120 Tons 10 Carriage Guns besides Swivals haveing men on board her Includeing the french Troops dureing the Engagement she Killed two of our people & wounded one, the Brigg had several wounded & seven Killed." She was brought to Halifax on 2 November.

29. See Vice Admiralty Proceedings.

30. CO 217/11, f. 3: Cornwallis to Board of Trade, 27 November 1750.
31. Capt. Edward Le Cras, master of the sloop *Tryal*.
32. Ship *Two Friends* does not arrive until 2 April.
33. Forty-fifth Regiment of Foot.
34. JS is proven wrong, below, on 26 March and 13 May.
35. Treacherous islands and ledges off the southern tip of Nova Scotia.
36. *OED*. Set in. To begin, become prevalent; chiefly of the weather entering upon a particular state.
37. CO 217/11, f. 22: Cornwallis to Board of Trade, 30 November 1750. JS had been paid £150.
38. CO 217/40, f. 312: La Jonquière to Cornwallis, 25 November 1750. In this letter, La Jonquière accuses Cornwallis of warlike acts, for which he desires an explanation or else, he threatens, "votre silence jointe A tous vos actes d'hostilitè me mettront dans la dure Necessitè d'user de Reprisailles sans aucun menagement."
39. CO 217/40, f. 308: Council minutes for 9 February 1750. The council heard a deposition from three individuals against Thomas Power, mariner, who was accused of having fired on a schooner in Torbay Harbour and having robbed it of a cable and anchor. Bail was set at £100.
40. Perhaps William Jeffray, later commissary of ordnance stores.
41. Power had been ordered to stand trial. See below, 4 June.
42. CO 217/11, f. 5. Probably Freeman Gunter, a local merchant who later became treasurer of Nova Scotia. Cornwallis wrote to the Board of Trade on 27 November 1750, "I have employd Mr Gunter a person Who has shewn his regard for the Settlement by laying Out a great deal of Money in it whereas the Others have not contributed a sixpence to it and have had the supplying I dare say one half of the necessarys wanted and this is the Return they make."
43. CO 217/40, f. 317. At the council meeting held 9 March 1750, the councillors took an oath of secrecy.
44. Cf. note 37, above.
45. Wilson, *A Genuine Narrative of the Transactions in Nova*

Scotia, pp. 15-20, describes the assault. He writes that "the Child who had been out of the way at the time of the Assault, missing his Father, went into the Woods in Quest of him, and having gone too far, one of the Maroders seized upon him, and taking out a large Knife, held him while another scalped him, amidst the most piercing Groans, and then made off leaving him as dead; here he continued in this Situation till next Morning, when, being recovered a little, he knew not where he was, or where to go; however hearing the signal Gun at *Hallifax*, and then the *Trevally, i.e.* the Drums beat, he directed his Rout by the Sound, and being but two Miles off, he came into the Town, where he exhibited, in his own Person as terrible a Spectacle as any I have been describing. . . . *Grant*, the Surgeon of the Place, . . . applied Linnen Clothes, plaister'd over with Grease; and afterwards covered with warm Flannels; in this Situation he continued for a Month, and began to recover by degrees, to the Astonishment of all who saw him."

46. Forty-seventh Regiment of Foot.

47. The Tantramar Marshes bordered Chignecto Bay, the site of Fort Lawrence and Beauséjour. Baie Verte and Fort Lawrence straddled the Isthmus of Chignecto.

48. *OED*. Blow off. Drive or carry away.

49. L. H. Gipson, *The British Empire Before the American Revolution*, (New York: Knopf, 1936–70) 3: 15–16, says that rum was the common beverage of practically all the laborers. Men asserted they could not withstand the rigors of their jobs or the seasons without it. It was the basis of trade with the southern colonies. An immense quantity of inferior fish was carried to the West Indies, where it was bought with specie. Molasses, which usually existed in great surplus, could be bought from the French sugar islands.

50. Cf. J. J. McCusker, "The Rum Trade and the Balance of Payments of the Thirteen Continental Colonies, 1650–1775" (Ph.D. diss., University of Pittsburgh, 1970).

51. Le Cras notes in the *Tryal*'s log, 11 April, "Tr^d. several times between Sambro & Chibucto Head At 4 bore away for y^e. Harbour."

52. See "An Act for granting a Bounty upon Fish and Oyl and for laying a Duty upon Spirituous Liquors as a Fund for the Payment thereof, and for effectually Securing the payment of the said Duty, made and passed in Council at Halifax the 29th: April 1751," CO 219/3, ff. 41–43. In this act it was proposed to pay sixpence for every quintal of fish salted and dried in the province for export, a bounty of twelvepence for every barrel of pickled fish and 2*s*. 6*d*. per barrel for whale, seal or fish oil. This would be paid for by a duty of sixpence per gallon on liquor, principally rum. See also 26 April, below.

53. *OED*. Maugre. In spite of. Perhaps also "Mauger."

54. Cornwallis.

Book 6

1. The firm of Samuel Wentworth was one of the most eminent firms in Boston. See John Wentworth, *The Wentworth Genealogy* (Boston: Little, Brown & Co., 1878), 1:175–76.

2. Cf. p. 107 above.

3. Probably Colin Drummond, who was made quartermaster of Lascelles's regiment on 16 August 1750.

4. The report of the boundary commissioners was not published until 1755.

5. Lieutenant William Arbuthnot of Clapham's company of rangers. He was granted sick leave in Boston on 25 September 1751.

6. John Webb & Co. were owners of the snow *Elizabeth*.

7. Siege tactics used by Marlborough in Flanders. For a more detailed account of this attack, see *Gentleman's Magazine* 21 (1751): 379, and *London Magazine* 20 (1751): 341.

8. George Foster was master of the *Sarah*.

9. In a similar manner, Edward How had been killed by Indians disguised as French.

10. Probably Capt. Lt. Thomas Lewis.

11. The Shubenacadie Lake System linked Dartmouth to the

Bay of Fundy via short portages and the Shubenacadie River, and JS had learned of the route from Minas to Halifax during the Chignecto expedition of 1750 (see British Library, *King's Topographical Collection,* 119:59-2-c).

12. *OED.* Souse. In a secondary sense, it can mean "to strike heavily or severely," and in the eighteenth century it could mean "to impose upon or swindle."

13. See JS's account of the Power case in his letter of April 1753.

14. WO 25/23, f. 141. Robert Porter was appointed judge advocate and commissary of musters, 1 May 1752.

15. Vice Admiralty Court Proceedings, PANS, RG 1, vol. 492, pp. 1-21. The snow *Peggy,* Henry Dunn master, was tried before the court on 5 June 1751.

16. Cornwallis was to lose not one councillor but two. CO 217/40, f. 369. He wrote on 16 February 1752, "Col. Horsman having His Majesty's leave to go home and M^r. Salusbury mine both Councillors of the Province has made it necessary for me to appoint two new ones 'till His Majesty's pleasure is known."

17. 3 July 1750.

18. Thomas Dove, captain of the sloop *Hound.*

19. Rous had been detained at Annapolis by a weak mainmast. He noted in his journal on 5 July, "The Carpenters Inspecting into the Conditions of the Masts & yards acquainted one he found the Main Mast towards the Head much decayed & Rotten in 5 Seperate holes 8 or 9 Ins through, on which I had a Survey by all the Officers, who reported to me, that the Mast was decay'd & not fit to be trusted too." Rous then employed his ship's company in cutting a new spar and replacing the old one, an operation that took from 7 to 15 July.

20. The *Speedwell* was one of several transports bringing European Protestants to settle in the province. Three shiploads had already arrived in 1750. For a complete account of this colonizing scheme, see Bell, *The "Foreigh Protestants" and the Settlement of Nova Scotia.*

21. The *Albany* journal puts the arrival date at 24 July.

22. See CO 219/3, ff. 53–55, "An Act laying a Duty of three pence p[r]. Gallon on Spirituous Liquors imported from the Neighbouring Colonies and to encourage the Distilling thereof in this Province and for granting a Bounty of Ten Shillings p Ton upon all Vessells or Boats built within the said Province, made and passed in Council at Halifax the 31:[st] July 1751."

23. Le Cras was forced to return. He noted in the ship's log on 20 July, " . . . Struck upon a Sunken Rock between Buring Island and the Eastern Shore, when we got Clear of it put the Helm a Starboard & brought up wth. both Bowers ahead in the Enterance of the little Passage, the Ulysses being got through made the Sig[l]. for her to come in again. at Noon struck Yards and Topmasts and got down Topg[t]. Yards. The Ship struck Three times on the above mentioned Rock and made a little Water at the time she struck." Le Cras took until 22 July to examine his hull, then returned to the dockyard in Halifax for repairs by 30 July.

24. On his way to Halifax on 29 July, Le Cras wrote, "At 7 am passed by a Large Ship w[ch]. we took to be a French Man of War of 60 or 70 Guns."

25. William Rickson was a captain in Lascelles's regiment.

26. According to the *Albany*'s log, the *Osborne* sailed on 6 August.

27. Foreign Protestants.

28. The point off the southern tip of England from which dead reckonings were measured by navigators.

Book 7

1. A hamlet in Hampshire, eight-and-a-half miles northeast of Petersfield. It was a well-known halting place for coaches traveling the old Portsmouth road.

2. A small port at the northwest extremity of Portsmouth harbor.

3. *Johnson*. Pipe. A liquid measure containing two hogsheads [about 105 imperial gallons].

4. The change from the Julian to the Gregorian Calendar was made that year, so that 2 September was followed by 14 September.

5. Captain James Young.

6. Balderston, ed., *Thraliana*, 1:294. "My Father now wrote [my mother] melancholly Letters too, telling how he had fought a Duel at Madera with Captn Young of the Sphinx [*sic*], for shewing Hopson (whom he hated)—more Civilities than him." See also JS's letter of 28 June 1752.

7. These dates substantially agree with those entered in the *Jason* log, except that the log shows the date of anchorage in Halifax as 28 July.

8. At this time, Otis Little was commissary of stores. At the council of 18 August 1752, JS was appointed to a committee that included Colonel Lawrence, Captain Fotheringham, Collier, and Steele. Cornwallis summoned Little, Bulkeley, Saul, Benjamin Gerrish (Townsend's agent), Cotterell, and William Magee and ordered an inquiry to be made into irregularities in provisioning the settlement. See CO 220/2, f. 194 f.

9. Chauncey Townshend, victualling contractor.

10. Christopher Kilby, a New Englander who became financial agent for Nova Scotia and who was responsible for dispensing parliamentary grants for the service of the colony.

11. Commissary of stores and provisions.

12. John Dick, a British merchant in Rotterdam who acted as agent for the procuring of "foreign Protestants."

13. About this time, the *Pearl* arrived with 212 passengers. See Bell, *The "Foreign Protestants,"* p.198.

14. Captain James Young.

15. John Allen, lieutenant of HMS *Jason*.

16. Council agreed to lay aside a scheme to issue the "foreign Protestants" threepence a day in lieu of provisions. See CO 217/13, f. 268f.: Hopson to Board of Trade, 16 October 1752.

17. Alderman William Baker was the colonial agent who contracted to victual the forces in Halifax.

18. Captain Cotterell was appointed to the council on 23 October and, for a time, acted as secretary of the province.

19. See "An Act For the Relief of Debtors, with Respect to

the Imprisonment of their Persons," CO 219/4, ff. 26–34. This act, drawn up by a committee of Green, Steele, and Collier, took notice that no provision was made for the maintenance of debtors in H.M. Gaol and that they depended for their lives on the charity of compassionate citizens. It provided a process for speeding up cases of this kind, but it also assigned to the creditor, if the prisoner were remanded, the responsibility of supplying "the full Quantity of Eight Pounds of good and wholesome Biscuit Bread per Week, unto the said Prisoner." It was enacted on 6 December 1752.

20. See p. 201, n. 4.

21. A peace agreement with the Micmacs was signed on 16 September. See CO 217/13, f. 306.

22. It appears that Collier had taken over the duties of register, though he was not appointed to that position until June 1753.

23. *OED*. Plunge. To overwhelm, especially with trouble or difficulty.

24. Sebastian Zouberbuhler.

25. CO 220/2, p. 213. On 25 September 1752, council authorized the borrowing of these provisions from Saul, who was Baker's agent, until the arrival of government stores.

26. CO 220/2, p. 226. The council of 3 October 1752 deferred passing the bill into law until the opinion of the Board of Trade had been received.

27. Governor Hopson. This term, cleverly chosen by JS from Aesop's fables, is full of satiric overtones. In the fable of King Log and King Stork, Jupiter sends a log to the frogs who have asked for a king. But when they complain of its inertness, he sends them a stork, which devours them. In this fable, as soon as the frogs notice that the log is harmless, they jump up and down upon it, then go about their business without noticing the king lying in their midst. The phrase "King Log" is not used in the popular edition *Fables of Aesop and Others* (1722) but is found in Alexander Pope's *Dunciad* (1728), 1:327–30.

28. JS uses this term to refer to the political situation in

Halifax. In Pope's *Dunicad*, 1:9–10, "Dulness o'er all possess'd her antient right,/Daughter of Chaos and eternal Night."

29. Lieutenant William Bryan of Leighton's regiment?

30. *OED*. Politian. One who studies or is expert in polity.

31. John Duport, an attorney who came out with Cornwallis and became a justice of the peace. In February 1752, he had also been made a judge of the Inferior Court of Common Pleas.

32. CO 220/2, pp. 227–28. Green presented his resignation to council on 10 October 1752, claiming that the duties had become too great for him, but he continued as a member of council.

33. Captain John Hamilton.

34. Probably 21 October, the date of Cornwallis's departure.

35. William Piggot came to Halifax from Louisbourg, where he had been granted a license to keep a "house of entertainment" in 1745. In Halifax he owned the schooners *Success* and *Fancy*, with which he continued to trade with Lewisbourg.

36. CO 220/2, p. 227. Major Cope had requested Piggot to confer with the Indians on behalf of the colony about coming to renew the peace. He was ordered by the council of 10 October 1752 to bring the Indians back with him.

37. See CO 217/40, ff. 379–83, copy of treaty signed by Hopson and Cope on 22 November 1752. The council promised to supply bread, flour, and other provisions half yearly as well as presents of blankets, tobacco, powder, and shot each year. The same treatment was promised any other tribe who would sign a similar treaty.

38. Ship's captain or Lieutenant Robert Armstrong of Shirley's regiment.

39. *OED*. Mulked. Punished by fine.

40. Hopson.

41. *Johnson*. Lurch. To defeat; to disappoint.

42. Combermere Abbey, the seat of Sir Lynch Salusbury Cotton.

43. London address of Sir Thomas Salusbury.
44. Council proposed a law to encourage settlers by forgiving their debts.
45. Probably Robert Grant, a Scottish merchant who later became a councillor.
46. *Johnson*. To trim. To balance; to fluctuate between two parties.
47. John Breynton.
48. The reasons for the colony's lack of success to this point are put more fully by Charles Morris in "Remarks concerning the settlement of Nova Scotia," British Library Add. MS 19,072, f. 2 ff.
49. JS gives a fuller account of the affair in the letter of April 1753. At the council of 5 April 1753, Thomas Power, who had been convicted of piracy, brought forward a complaint against Monk. Although the charge of fraud was not proved conclusively, Monk's actions were considered unworthy of a member of the court, and he was given a reprimand that took note that he had been suspected previously. Otis Little, for his part in the affair, was dismissed from the office of king's advocate. See CO 220/3, pp. 195–203.
50. The remainder of the journal is written on five loose pages, the first of which is numbered "two," and this accounts for the hiatus here. To maintain the sequence of events, I have not followed the numbering of the pages.
51. JS attended his last council on 16 April.
52. CO 218/4, f. 220–21. These steps had already been taken, but the letter from the Board of Trade was not written until 28 March.
53. CO 217/14, f. 151. In Hopson's letter to the Board of Trade, 16 April, JS is named as the bearer of a letter to England.

Appendix A

1. See *London Gazette*, 22–25 April 1749. The *Beaufort, Canning, London*, and *Everley* were loaded 24–27 April at

Long Reach and Tower Wharf, London, before sailing on the first leg of the journey.

2. The *Albany* journal shows that Rous did not sail until 26 July, and JS did not go.

3. Sounds.

4. According to the 1740 *Army List*, Hans Fowler was commissioned an ensign in Lieutenant-General Kirke's Regiment of Foot in 1736. JS was a cousin of the Fowlers by marriage. See below, p. 145.

5. Richard Lloyd, the companion and business agent of JS. See *Boswell's Life of Johnson*, ed. G. B. Hill (Oxford: Clarendon Press, 1934-50; 1964), 6:594.

6. Bach–y–graig.

7. Forty-seventh Regiment of Foot.

8. Shropshire.

9. Boston merchant.

10. Hester's mother.

11. Traeth Mawr. Estuarial bay at the mouth of the river Madoc, on the border between Carnarvon and Merioneth.

12. See above, p. 92, n. 32. At Tan–y–Blwch there was an inn frequented by Welsh tourists.

13. *OED*. Cag. A small cask.

14. JS's manservant.

15. Bedfordshire town.

16. James Johnson was married to Lord Halifax's daughter. He was promoted to the rank of lieutenant-colonel in the Royal Regiment of Horse Guards on 17 December 1754.

17. *Johnson*. Event. The consequence of an action; the conclusion; the upshot.

18. Perhaps Captain John Major, the agent for the ships taken up by the Commissioners of the Navy for transporting settlers to Nova Scotia or Joshua Mauger.

19. Halifax did not leave the Board of Trade until 1761.

20. Dr. Charles Pinfold was an advocate to the Lords of the Admiralty and an old friend of JS from his university days.

21. Sedgwick, Romney, ed., *The House of Commons, 1715-1754* (London: H.M. Stationery Office, 1970), 1:586: "The Cottons were one of the leading Whig families in

Cheshire. In September 1749, Sir Watkin Williams Wynn, M.P. for Denbighshire, died, and [Sir Lynch] Cotton wrote to Richard Myddelton, M.P. for Denbigh boroughs, pledging his support. Myddelton was seeking a peerage, and preferred to hold the boroughs uncontested. So an agreement was reached under which Cotton was unanimously nominated for the county, for which he was returned unopposed. This arrangement continued until he retired in 1774.''

22. John Wynn, M.P. for Denbigh boroughs, 1741–47.

23. William Bodvell, M.P. for Carnarvonshire, 1741–54.

24. H. A. Herbert, head of the Shropshire Whigs, was created Lord Herbert of Chirbury in 1743. He became Earl of Powis on the death of a distant cousin in 1748. It was he who negotiated the seat for William Bodvell in 1741, and Bodvell thus became one of the Powis group in the Commons.

25. The *Montagu*, after Lord Halifax's family name.

26. *OED*. Determine. To put an end to.

27. While Power was on trial, his wife was approached by Monk, who prevailed upon her to sell him their house and lot for £300. He argued that Power would certainly be hanged and that consequently the house and lot would be forfeited. She would avoid this by selling before the trial began. Monk also advised her to seek legal assistance from Otis Little, who accepted £10 from her even though he was acting for the prosecution.

Bibliography

1. Manuscripts

This section includes only a selection of the manuscript collections consulted. For a fuller description, readers should refer to the valuable bibliographies produced by writers of colonial history, particularly those published in recent years for the *Dictionary of Canadian Biography*. Rather than writing history, I have been engaged in the narrower business of arranging facts, identifying forgotten people, locating remote places, and dredging up details of the daily round. What appears below is meant only as a guide to those engaged in similar work.

The richest collection of official records surviving from the period is held by the Public Record Office in London (available on microfilm at the Public Archives of Canada). CO 217 to 220 are particularly useful, for they contain the original correspondence between colonial governors and the Lords Commissioners of Trade and Plantations as well as sessional papers, commissions and instructions, acts, shipping returns for the port of Halifax, and much else. PRO 30/50/39 contains three additional letters from Hugh Davidson to Richard Neville Aldworth, undersecretary of state to the duke of Bedford. Naval and military commissions appear in ADM 6/16–18 and in WO 25/22–24, 25/90. Many original ships' logs containing details of voyages to Nova Scotia and along the coasts are to be found in ADM 51 (captains) and ADM 52 (masters). The lieutenants' logs, however, form part of the ADM/L series at the National Maritime Museum, Greenwich. At the British Library, the Egerton, Hardwicke, and Newcastle manuscripts contain other related correspondence, and in the *King's Topographical Collection*, vol. 119, there is a valuable collection of maps and sketches showing various parts of Nova Scotia as it was when Salusbury's journal was written. Reports from missionaries are preserved by the United Society for the Propagation of the Gospel. The journal itself (Rylands Eng. MS 615) forms part of the vast collection of Salusbury papers—correspondence, charters, business documents—in the John Rylands University Library of Manchester. The Rylands manuscript catalogue gives a detailed description of this collection, as does Moses Tyson's "Unpublished Manuscripts, Papers and Letters of Dr. Johnson, Mrs. Thrale, and Their Friends in the John Rylands Library," *Bulletin of the John Rylands Library*, 15 (1931): 467–88.

In Halifax, N.S., many original records from the first years of the settlement may still be found at the Public Archives of Nova Scotia (PANS), and others, such as the papers of the Fortieth Regiment, have been copied or microfilmed for local use. For my purpose, I have found particularly useful the Saint Paul's Church register (1749–1835); the Vice Admiralty Court records; books of accounts transacted with sloops of war; governors' commissions, licenses and warrants; the census of 1752, and the Monk papers. The Crown Lands office of the provincial government of Nova Scotia is still in possession of John Salusbury's original registry book as well as the first allotment book and escheatment book and the plans for the original layout of Halifax and the adjoining areas, showing the names of the original grantees.

2. Printed Books

This section contains only those works quoted or cited and those directly related to the settlement of Halifax or John Salusbury's family. For the sake of brevity, I have excluded general historical studies and such standard reference works as the *Dictionary of Canadian Biography*.

(a) Primary Sources

Akins, T. B., ed. *Selections from the Public Documents of the Province of Nova Scotia*. Halifax: C. Annand, 1869.

Army List. Published first in 1740, second in 1754, and annually throughout the eighteenth century.

"J. B." and "W. M." *An Account of the Present State of Nova-Scotia: in Two Letters to a Noble Lord: One from a Gentleman in the Navy lately arrived from thence. The other from a Gentleman who long resided there.* London, 1756.

Burke, Edmund. *Speech of Edmund Burke, Esq. Member of Parliament for the City of Bristol, On presenting to the House of Commons (On the 11th of February, 1780) A Plan for the Better Security of the Independence of Parliament, and the Oeconomical Reformation of the Civil and other Establishments.* London, 1780.

Cumberland, Richard. *Memoirs.* London: Printed for Lackington, Allen, and Co., 1806.

de Forest, L. E., ed. *Louisbourg Journals, 1745.* New York: Society of Colonial Wars, 1932.

Des Barres, J. F. W. *The Atlantic Neptune, Published for the use of the Royal Navy of Great Britain, By Joseph F. W. Des Barres Esq., Under the Direction of the Right Honble. The Lords Commissioners of the Admiralty. . . .* 5 vols. London, 1776–80.

Douglass, William, M.D. *A Summary, Historical and Political, of the First Planting, Progressive Improvements, and Present State of the British Settlements in North-America.* 2 vols. London, 1760.

An Essay On The Present State Of The Province of Nova-Scotia, With some Strictures on the Measures pursued by Government from its first Settlement by the English in the Year, 1749. [London, 1774?].

"Extract of a Plan presented to His Majesty by the Earl of Halifax for the Settlement of His Majesty's Colony of Nova Scotia," in *Report of the Board of Trustees of the Public Archives of Nova Scotia for the Year 1971,* pp. 21-50. Halifax: Public Archives of Nova Scotia, 1971.

Fergusson, C. Bruce, ed. *Minutes of His Majesty's Council at Annapolis Royal, 1736-1749.* Halifax: Public Archives of Nova Scotia, 1967.

Gay, John. *Fables.* 5th ed. London, 1737.

Gentleman's Magazine. London, 1731-1907.

A Genuine Account of Nova Scotia: Containing, A Description of its Situation, Air, Climate, Soil and its Produce;

also *Rivers, Bays, Harbours, and Fish, with which they abound in very great Plenty.* London and Dublin, 1750.

A Geographic History of Nova Scotia, Containing an Account of the Situation, Extent and Limits thereof. London, 1749.

Gilroy, Marion, comp. "A Catalogue of Maps, Plans and Charts in the Public Archives of Nova Scotia," *Bulletin of the Public Archives of Nova Scotia* 1, no. 3. Halifax: Public Archives of Nova Scotia, 1938.

Grenville, Richard. *The Grenville Papers: Being the Correspondence of Richard Grenville Earl Temple, K.G., and the Right Hon: George Grenville, Their Friends and Contemporaries.* Edited by William James Smith. 4 vols. London: John Murray, 1852–53.

Halifax Gazette. Halifax, 1752–66.

Hervey, Lord John. *Some Material Towards Memoirs of the Reign of King George II.* Edited by Romney Sedgwick. 3 vols. London: Eyre and Spottiswoode, 1931.

[Hollingsworth, S.]. *An Account of the Present State of Nova Scotia.* Edinburgh, 1786.

The Importance of Settling and Fortifying Nova Scotia: with A Particular Account of the Climate, Soil and Native Inhabitants of the Country. By a Gentleman lately arrived from that Colony. London, 1751.

[Jefferys, Thomas]. *The Conduct of the French, With Regard to Nova Scotia; From its first Settlement to the present Time.* In which are exposed the Falsehood and Absurdity of their Arguments made use of to elude the Force of the Treaty of UTRECHT, and support their unjust Proceedings. In a Letter to a Member of Parliament. London, 1755.

Johnson, Samuel. *A Dictionary of the English Language.* London, 1755.

Journal of the Commissioners for Trade and Plantations. 12 vols. London: H. M. Stationery Office, 1936.

[Little, Otis]. *The State of Trade in the Northern Colonies Considered; With An Account of their Produce, And a particular Description of Nova Scotia.* London, 1748.

London Gazette. London, 1666-[in progress].

London Magazine. London, 1732-85.

MacMechan, Archibald M., ed. *A Calendar of Two Letter-Books and One Commission-Book in the Possession of the Government of Nova Scotia, 1713–1741.* Halifax: Herald Printing House, 1900.

———, ed. *Original Minutes of His Majesty's Council at Annapolis Royal, 1720–1739.* Halifax: McAlpine Publishing Co., 1908.

The Memorials of the English and French Commissaries Concerning the Limits of Nova Scotia or Acadia. London, 1755.

Morris, Charles. "Description and State of the New Settlements in Nova Scotia in 1761, by the Chief Surveyor," in *Report Concerning Canadian Archives for the Year 1904,* pp. 287–300. Ottawa: King's Printer. 1905.

———. "Report by Captain Morris to Governor Shirley upon His Survey of Lands in Nova Scotia Available for Protestant Settlers, 1749," in *Report of the Work of the Archives Branch for the Year 1912,* pp. 79–83. Ottawa: King's Printer, 1913.

The Northcliffe Collection. Ottawa: King's Printer, 1926.

The Nova Scotia's Garland; Furnished with Three merry New Songs. [Newcastle, ?1750].

Piozzi, Hester Lynch. *Thraliana: The Diary of Mrs. Hester Lynch Thrale (Later Mrs. Piozzi).* Edited by Katherine C. Balderston. 2 vols. 2d ed. Oxford: Clarendon Press, 1951.

———. *Anecdotes of Samuel Johnson.* Edited by S. C. Roberts. Cambridge: University Press, 1932.

———. *Dr. Johnson's Mrs. Thrale. Autobiography, Letters and Literary Remains of Mrs. Piozzi.* Edited by A. Hayward and J. H. Lobban. Edinburgh and London: T. N. Foulis, 1910.

Pope, Alexander. *The Dunciad.* Twickenham Edition of The Poems of Alexander Pope, vol. 5. Edited by James Sutherland. London: Methuen, 1943.

Salusbury, Sir John, and Robert Chester. *Poems.* Introd. Carleton Brown. Early English Text Society, Extra Series, no. 113. London: Kegan Paul, Trench, Trübner and Co., Ltd., and Oxford University Press, 1914.

Shortt, Adam, V. K. Johnson, and Gustave Lanctot, eds. *Documents Relating to Currency, Exchange and Finance in Nova Scotia with Prefatory Documents, 1675-1758. Ottawa: King's Printer, 1933.

Smythies, Capt. R. H. Raymond. *Historical Records of the 40th (2nd Somersetshire) Regiment, Now 1st Battalion the Prince of Wales's Volunteers (South Lancashire Regiment.) From its Formation, in 1717, to 1893.* Devonport: Printed for the Subscribers by A. H. Swiss, 1894.

The Spectator. Edited by Donald F. Bond. 5 vols. Oxford: Clarendon Press, 1965.

"J. W." *A Letter From a Gentleman in Nova-Scotia, to A Person of Distinction on the Continent. Describing the present State of Government in that Colony. With some seasonable Remarks.* [London?], 1756.

Webster, J. C., ed. *The Journal of Joshua Winslow.* Historical Studies No. 2. St. John, N.B.: Publications of the New Brunswick Museum, 1936.

―――. *Journals of Beauséjour.* Diary of John Thomas. Journal of Louis de Courville. Halifax: Public Archives of Nova Scotia, 1937.

―――. *The Building of Fort Lawrence in Chignecto.* A Journal Recently Found in the Gates Collection, New York Historical Society. Historical Studies No. 2. Saint John, N.B.: Publications of the New Brunswick Museum, 1941.

Willard, Abijah. "Journal of Abijah Willard of Lancaster, Mass., An Officer in the Expedition which captured Fort Beauséjour in 1755," *Collections of the New Brunswick Historical Society* 13 (1930): 3-75.

Wilson, John. *A Genuine Narrative of the Transactions in Nova Scotia, Since the Settlement, June 1749, till August the 5th, 1751; In which the Nature, Soil, and Produce of the Country are related, with the particular Attempts of the Indians to disturb the Colony.* By John Wilson, Late Inspector of Stores. London, [1751?].

(b) Secondary Sources

Adshead, J. G. "Hon. John Salusbury, 1707-62," *Collections of the Nova Scotia Historical Society* 29 (1951): 1-21.

Akins, T. B. "The First Council," *Collections of the Nova Scotia Historical Society* 2 (1881): 17–30.

———, ed. *Acadia and Nova Scotia*. Documents relating to the Acadian French and the first British colonization of the Province, 1714–58. Halifax: Charles Annand, 1869.

———. *History of Halifax City*. Halifax: Nova Scotia Historical Society, 1895.

Armit, W. B. *Halifax, 1749–1906: Soldiers Who Founded and Garrisoned a Famous City*. Public Archives of Nova Scotia, unpublished manuscript [1962].

Ballinger, Sir John. "Katheryn of Berain," *Y Cymmrodor* 40 (1929): 1–42.

Barnstead, Arthur S. "Development of the Office of Provincial Secretary, Nova Scotia," *Collections of the Nova Scotia Historical Society* 24 (1938): 1–31.

Basye, A. H. *The Lords Commissioners of Trade and Plantations*. Yale Historical Studies No. 3, Miscellany XIV. New Haven, Conn.: Yale University Press, 1925.

Bates, George T. "The Great Exodus of 1749, or, the Cornwallis Settlers Who Didn't," *Collections of the Nova Scotia Historical Society* 38 (1973): 27–62.

Baxter, W. T. *The House of Hancock, Business in Boston 1724–1775*. New York: Russell and Russell, 1945.

Beck, J. Murray. *The Government of Nova Scotia*. Toronto: University of Toronto Press, 1957.

Bell, Winthrop P. *The "Foreign Protestants" and the Settlement of Nova Scotia*. Toronto: University of Toronto Press, 1961.

Boswell, James. *Boswell's Life of Johnson*. Edited by G. B. Hill; revised by L. F. Powell. 6 vols Oxford: Clarendon Press, 1934–50; 1964.

Brebner, J. B. *New England's Outpost*. New York: Columbia University Press, 1927.

Broadley, A. M. *Doctor Johnson and Mrs. Thrale*. London: John Lane The Bodley Head, 1910.

Calnek, W. A. *History of the County of Annapolis*. Toronto: William Briggs, 1897.

Chard, Donald F. "The Impact of Île Royale On New England, 1713-1763" Ph.D. dissertation, University of Ottawa, 1976.

Clark, Andrew H. *Acadia: The Geography of Early Nova Scotia to 1760*. Madison, Wisc.: University of Winsconsin Press, 1968.

Clifford, J. L. *Hester Lynch Piozzi (Mrs. Thrale)*. 2d ed. Oxford: Clarendon Press, 1952.

[Cokayne, George E., ed.] *Complete Baronetage*. 5 vols. Exeter: W. Pollard and Co., 1900-06.

Douglas, W. A. B. "The Sea Militia of Nova Scotia, 1749-1755: A Comment on Naval Policy," *Canadian Historical Review* 47 (1966): 22-37.

———, "Nova Scotia and the Royal Navy, 1713-1766." Ph.D. dissertation, Queen's University, 1973.

Eatson, A. W. H. *Lt.-Col. Otho Hamilton of Olivestob . . . His Sons, Captain John and Lieutenant-Colonel Otho Hamilton, 2ND, and His Grandson, Sir Ralph Hamilton, Kt*. Halifax: Ruggles, 1899.

Fergusson, C. Bruce, ed. *A Directory of the Members of the Legislative Assembly of Nova Scotia, 1758-1958*. Halifax: Public Archives of Nova Scotia, 1958.

Fisher, Lewis R., "Revolution without Independence: The Halifax Merchants and the American Revolution." Ph.D. dissertation, York University, 1979.

Fraser, D. G. L. "The Origin and Function of the Court of Vice Admiralty in Halifax 1749-1759," *Collections of the Nova Scotia Historical Society* 33 (1961): 57-80.

Gipson, L.H. *The British Empire Before the American Revolution*. 15 vols. New York: Knopf, 1936-70.

Harris, Reginald V. *The Church of Saint Paul in Halifax, Nova Scotia: 1749-1949*. Toronto: Ryerson, 1949.

Henretta, James A. *"Salutary Neglect": Colonial Administration Under the Duke of Newcastle*. Princeton, N.J.: Princeton University Press, 1972.

Hutton, Elizabeth A. "The Micmac Indians of Nova Scotia to 1834." M.A. thesis, Dalhousie University, 1961.

Hyde, Mary. *The Thrales of Streatham Park*. Cambridge, Mass.: Harvard University Press, 1977.

Laing, Lionel H. "Nova Scotia's Admiralty Court as a Problem of Colonial Administration," *Canadian Historical Review* 16 (1935): 151-61.

Lawson, Mrs. William. *History of the Townships of Dartmouth, Preston and Lawrenceton*. Halifax: Morton and Co., 1893.

McCusker, John J. "The Rum Trade and the Balance of Payments of the Thirteen Continental Colonies, 1650-1775." Ph.D. dissertation, University of Pittsburgh, 1970.

Mackinnon, Ian F. *Settlements and Churches in Nova Scotia. 1749-1776*. Halifax, [1930].

McLennan, J. S. *Louisbourg, From Its Foundation to Its Fall*. London: Macmillan, 1918.

MacMechan, Archibald M. "Ab Urbe Condite," *Dalhousie Review* 7 (1927): 198-210.

MacNutt, W. S. "Why Halifax Was Founded," *Dalhousie Review* 12 (1932): 524-32.

———. "The Beginnings of Nova Scotian Politics, 1758-1766," *Canadian Historical Review* 16 (1935): 41-53.

Murdoch, Beamish. *A History of Nova Scotia, or Acadie*. 3 vols. Halifax: James Barnes, 1865-67.

Pargellis, Staneley, ed. *Military Affairs in North America, 1748-1765*. [Hamden, Conn.]: Archon Books, 1969.

Parsons, Usher. *The Life of Sir William Pepperrell, Bart*. Boston: Little, Brown, 1855.

Paulson, Ronald. *Hogarth: His Life, Art, and Times*. 2 vols. New Haven, Conn.: Yale University Press, 1971.

Piers, Harry. *The Evolution of the Halifax Fortress, 1749-1928*. Halifax: Public Archives of Nova Scotia, 1947.

Punch, Terrence M. "The Halifax Connection, 1749-1848: A Century of Oligarchy in Nova Scotia." M.A. thesis, St. Mary's University, 1972.

Raddall, Thomas H. "The Feast of St. Aspinquid," *Nova Scotia Historical Quarterly* 1 (1971): 1-9.

———. *Roger Sudden*. Toronto: McClelland, 1944.

Rawlyk, George A. *Nova Scotia's Massachusetts, A Study of Massachusetts-Nova Scotia Relations, 1630-1784*. Montreal and London: McGill-Queen's Press, 1973.

Raymond, Rev. W. O. "Nova Scotia under English Rule; from the Capture of Port Royal to the Conquest of Canada, A.D. 1710-1760," *Transactions of the Royal Society of Canada* 4, sect. 2 (1910): 55-84.

Rompkey, Ronald. "Mrs. Hester Thrale (Piozzi) and the Pursuit of her 'Nova Scotia Fortune'," *Dalhousie Review* 58 (1978): 434-42.

Savelle, Max. *The Diplomatic History of the Canadian Boundary*

1749–1763. New Haven: Yale University Press, 1940.

Sedgwick, Romney. *The House of Commons, 1715–1754*. London: H. M. Stationery Office, 1970.

Smith, A. Tanner. "Transportation and Communication In Nova Scotia, 1749–1815." M.A. thesis, Dalhousie University, 1936.

Smith, W. J., ed. *Calendar of Salusbury Correspondence, 1553– circa 1700*. Board of Celtic Studies, University of Wales History and Law Series, No. XIV. Cardiff: University of Wales Press, 1954.

Venn, John, and J. A. Venn, comps. *Alumni Catabrigienses. A Biographical List of all Known Students . . . from the Earliest Times to 1900*. Two parts in 10 vols. Cambridge: University Press, 1922–54.

Ward, W. Peter. "The Acadian Response to the Growth of British Power in Nova Scotia, 1749–1755," *Dalhousie Review* 51 (1971): 165–77.

Wentworth, John. *The Wentworth Genealogy*. Boston: Little, Brown, and Co., 1878.

Williams, Katherine R. "Social Conditions in Nova Scotia, 1749–1783." M.A. thesis, McGill University, 1936.

Index

217